CONTENTS

Chapter 1 Terror and Violent Extremism

Terrorist or extremist activity	1
The changing face of terrorism	2
7/7: five years on	4
On the fifth anniversary of the 7/7 London transit attack	5
Islamist terrorism	8
Groomed for suicide: how Taliban recruits children for mass murder	11
Half of secondary heads seek police help on violent extremism	12
Animal rights extremists 'more of a problem than Islamists'	13
Irish Republican terrorist groups	14

Chapter 2 Tackling Terrorism

Anti-terrorism powers	15
Should Britain work with 'extremists' to prevent terrorism?	17
The Terrorism Acts – the facts	19
Terrorism Prevention and Investigation Measures Bill	20
The counter-terrorism review	21
Al-Qaeda will seek revenge	23
Victory in the war on terror is now within the West's reach	24

Chapter 3 Liberty vs Security

Stop trying to balance liberty with security	26
Only one in four terror suspects charged	27
Stop and search figures 'hide evidence of systematic anti-Muslim discrimination'	28
Searchlight on religion	30
Misconceptions about Islam and terrorism	32
Guantánamo Bay: now's the time for Barack Obama to close it down	33
Guantánamo Bay detainees are not ordinary criminals	34
Testimonies from detainees	36
The United Kingdom fails on diplomatic assurances	38
Key Facts	40
Glossary	41
Index	42
Acknowledgements	43
Assignments	44

OTHER TITLES IN THE ISSUES SERIES

For more on these titles, visit: www.independence.co.uk

Sustainability and Environment ISBN 978 1 86168 419 6
A Classless Society? ISBN 978 1 86168 422 6
Migration and Population ISBN 978 1 86168 423 3
Sexual Orientation and Society
ISBN 978 1 86168 440 0
The Gender Gap ISBN 978 1 86168 441 7
Domestic Abuse ISBN 978 1 86168 442 4
Travel and Tourism ISBN 978 1 86168 443 1
The Problem of Globalisation
ISBN 978 1 86168 444 8
The Internet Revolution ISBN 978 1 86168 451 6
An Ageing Population ISBN 978 1 86168 452 3
Poverty and Exclusion ISBN 978 1 86168 453 0
Waste Issues ISBN 978 1 86168 454 7
Staying Fit ISBN 978 1 86168 455 4
Drugs in the UK ISBN 978 1 86168 456 1
The AIDS Crisis ISBN 978 1 86168 468 4
Bullying Issues ISBN 978 1 86168 469 1
Marriage and Cohabitation ISBN 978 1 86168 470 7
Our Human Rights ISBN 978 1 86168 471 4
Privacy and Surveillance ISBN 978 1 86168 472 1
The Animal Rights Debate ISBN 978 1 86168 473 8
Body Image and Self-Esteem ISBN 978 1 86168 484 4
Abortion – Rights and Ethics ISBN 978 1 86168 485 1
Racial and Ethnic Discrimination ISBN 978 1 86168 486 8
Sexual Health ISBN 978 1 86168 487 5
Selling Sex ISBN 978 1 86168 488 2
Citizenship and Participation ISBN 978 1 86168 489 9
Health Issues for Young People ISBN 978 1 86168 500 1
Crime in the UK ISBN 978 1 86168 501 8
Reproductive Ethics ISBN 978 1 86168 502 5
Tackling Child Abuse ISBN 978 1 86168 503 2
Money and Finances ISBN 978 1 86168 504 9
The Housing Issue ISBN 978 1 86168 505 6
Teenage Conceptions ISBN 978 1 86168 523 0
Work and Employment ISBN 978 1 86168 524 7
Understanding Eating Disorders ISBN 978 1 86168 525 4
Student Matters ISBN 978 1 86168 526 1
Cannabis Use ISBN 978 1 86168 527 8
Health and the State ISBN 978 1 86168 528 5
Tobacco and Health ISBN 978 1 86168 539 1
The Homeless Population ISBN 978 1 86168 540 7
Coping with Depression ISBN 978 1 86168 541 4
The Changing Family ISBN 978 1 86168 542 1
Bereavement and Grief ISBN 978 1 86168 543 8
Endangered Species ISBN 978 1 86168 544 5
Responsible Drinking ISBN 978 1 86168 555 1
Alternative Medicine ISBN 978 1 86168 560 5

Censorship Issues ISBN 978 1 86168 558 2
Living with Disability ISBN 978 1 86168 557 5
Sport and Society ISBN 978 1 86168 559 9
Self-Harming and Suicide ISBN 978 1 86168 556 8
Sustainable Transport ISBN 978 1 86168 572 8
Mental Wellbeing ISBN 978 1 86168 573 5
Child Exploitation ISBN 978 1 86168 574 2
The Gambling Problem ISBN 978 1 86168 575 9
The Energy Crisis ISBN 978 1 86168 576 6
Nutrition and Diet ISBN 978 1 86168 577 3
Coping with Stress ISBN 978 1 86168 582 7
Consumerism and Ethics ISBN 978 1 86168 583 4
Genetic Modification ISBN 978 1 86168 584 1
Education and Society ISBN 978 1 86168 585 8
The Media ISBN 978 1 86168 586 5
Biotechnology and Cloning ISBN 978 1 86168 587 2
International Terrorism ISBN 978 1 86168 592 6
The Armed Forces ISBN 978 1 86168 593 3
Vegetarian Diets ISBN 978 1 86168 594 0
Religion in Society ISBN 978 1 86168 595 7
Tackling Climate Change ISBN 978 1 86168 596 4
Euthanasia and Assisted Suicide ISBN 978 1 86168 597 1

A note on critical evaluation

Because the information reprinted here is from a number of different sources, readers should bear in mind the origin of the text and whether the source is likely to have a particular bias when presenting information (just as they would if undertaking their own research). It is hoped that, as you read about the many aspects of the issues explored in this book, you will critically evaluate the information presented. It is important that you decide whether you are being presented with facts or opinions. Does the writer give a biased or an unbiased report? If an opinion is being expressed, do you agree with the writer?

International Terrorism offers a useful starting point for those who need convenient access to information about the many issues involved. However, it is only a starting point. Following each article is a URL to the relevant organisation's website, which you may wish to visit for further information.

Terrorist or extremist activity

Get the facts.

What is terrorism and violent extremist activity?

Trying to define terrorism can be difficult and controversial, because so many people and countries see it differently. But any definition usually includes:

⇨ mass intimidation – trying to make lots of people scared to go about their everyday or normal life;

⇨ unlawful violence or the threat of violence against the public;

⇨ violence intended to change a law, culture or political system, or to change how people think or act.

Having extreme thoughts or beliefs is not a crime. Using unlawful force or threats to support a belief or ideology is.

These criminal acts can include threatening someone because they are a different race, religion or sexual orientation; causing damage to property to get a political point of view across; or setting off a bomb to kill or injure people.

Case studies

Case study 1

On 7 July 2005 four men set off home-made bombs on three London underground trains and a bus, killing 52 people and injuring over 700 more. The bombers were also killed.

Case study 2

In September 2009 a 44-year-old man from Reading, Berkshire, was found guilty of terrorist-related offences after amassing components and material at his home which could be used to make incendiary and explosive devices. He had also collected far-right extremist material.

Case study 3

In January 2009 seven animal rights extremists were jailed for their part in a campaign to intimidate and blackmail people connected with an animal testing company. The campaign included sending letters to workers threatening violence against their children.

Why does terrorism or violent extremism happen?

There are many reasons to explain why it may happen but whatever the excuse is, these are criminal acts that cannot be justified under any circumstances.

> *Trying to define terrorism can be difficult and controversial, because so many people... see it differently*

Why do people get involved in terrorism or violent extremism?

There are many reasons why this may happen. Here are just some:

⇨ a lack of identity or belonging;

⇨ insecurity;

⇨ defending their culture, way of life or beliefs;

⇨ they may be pressured, or bullied into it;

⇨ they may have been radicalised by violent extremist groups;

⇨ they may want retaliation.

Those who encourage or get others to commit acts of violent extremism often target vulnerable people who are led into believing that violence or criminality can earn respect, riches or even glory.

However, even though a person may feel angry about something they believe is unfair this does not mean they should attack or threaten any person or any community.

Who are terrorists or violent extremists?

They can come from any background, any community, or any religion or belief. They can be young or old, male or female, rich or poor. They believe that violence or terrorism is an acceptable way of changing how others think or behave.

⇨ Information from the Metropolitan Police Authority. Visit www.safe.met.police.uk for more.

© *Metropolitan Police Authority 2011*

METROPOLITAN POLICE AUTHORITY

The changing face of terrorism

The modern terrorist knows no limits, says Professor Max Taylor, director of the Centre for the Study of Terrorism and Political Violence (CSTPV) at the University of St. Andrews, the first faculty of its kind in Europe.

Riots and malicious damage, sabotage and disruption, revolutions and assassinations: political violence in one shape or another has been with us since the earliest days of civilisation.

But at the extreme end of the political violence spectrum, terrorism is becoming increasingly bloody – and indiscriminate. And we may not have seen the worst of it yet, according to one expert.

Professor Max Taylor, director of the Centre for the Study of Terrorism and Political Violence (CSTPV) at the University of St. Andrews, has studied the subject for over 20 years. His publications include *The Future of Terrorism* and *The Fanatics: A Behavioural Approach To Political Violence.*

He thinks that extreme political violence has changed in two important ways. In the early days of terrorism, terrorists deliberated carefully over their targets. 'There would have been concern about victims – if it was appropriate to kill, who to kill, the circumstances and the death of civilians,' he says. 'The early European terrorists agonised over killing civilians but this soon receded as a concern… increasingly what we now see is not simply deaths of civilians but attempts at mass casualty rates.'

NOT THE SORT OF NEIGHBOURS I'D WANT!

The second important change in terrorist behaviour, Professor Taylor points out, is the use of suicide as a means of attack: 'Generally in European terrorism, escape for the terrorist was a rate-limiting factor. Recent experience has changed this.'

From activism to mass murder

The increasing use of suicide bombs or other extreme acts as a form of terrorism is often put down to brainwashing or indoctrination. But how does political dissent turn into radicalisation – and what do media pundits mean when they talk about 'breeding grounds' for terrorism?

Factors that contribute to political dissent are reasonably well-known – Professor Taylor cites social disadvantage, strong ideology and leadership. But it is much more difficult to identify the circumstances under which politically engaged people progress from political activism or association, to engaging in violence, he adds.

'Association with a radical group, for example, sounds like an obvious and critical element. But if you look at the so called "homegrown terrorists" they seem to have little direct involvement with such groups,' he says. 'I think we need to look much more towards psychological rather than political explanations for this – and by psychological I mean individual and idiosyncratic accounts, not psychopathology.'

Professor Taylor believes that political violence and terrorism is increasingly indiscriminate and therefore 'worse' than in the past because attacks are magnified by the media.

'If terrorism is about theatre then media attention magnifies its effects, and also its attractions… We seem to have lost a sense of "limits" to violence which I think is very worrying,' he explains. 'The ultimate fear is the use of weapons of mass destruction by terrorists. If the effects of mass casualties is an aspiration, the use of WMD seems to be an inevitable development.'

Does terrorism work?

The detonation of a dirty bomb in an urban environment would certainly be a game-changing atrocity for any terrorist. Suicide attacks such as those seen in Mumbai and London have only made everyday activities more difficult for the terrorists' perceived enemy, without fundamentally changing people's way of life.

LLOYD'S

Authorities' response to terrorism has made using public transport more time-consuming and fraught; opening a bank account is more complicated; even taking photographs of iconic architecture can risk an encounter with security staff.

More far-reaching changes to human rights have resulted, however. 'We have changed some of our legal assumptions, notions of due process, judicial imprisonment, and the way in which, for example, torture has been used against suspected terrorists. These are insults to the fundamental qualities of our way of life,' Professor Taylor states.

Suicide attacks such as those seen in Mumbai and London have only made everyday activities more difficult for the terrorists' perceived enemy, without fundamentally changing people's way of life

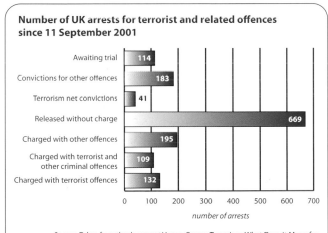

Number of UK arrests for terrorist and related offences since 11 September 2001

	number of arrests
Awaiting trial	114
Convictions for other offences	183
Terrorism net convictions	41
Released without charge	669
Charged with other offences	195
Charged with terrorist and other criminal offences	109
Charged with terrorist offences	132

Source: Taken from the document Home-Grown Terrorism: What Does it Mean for Business?, *produced by Lloyd's. These statistics are compiled from police records by the offices of the National Coordinator for Terrorist Investigations. They are subject to change as cases go through the system, and can be found at www.homeoffice.gov.uk/security/terrorism-and-the-aw/?version=3. Crown copyright*

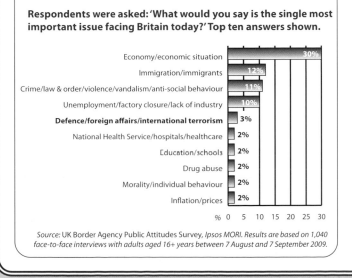

Respondents were asked: 'What would you say is the single most important issue facing Britain today?' Top ten answers shown.

	%
Economy/economic situation	30%
Immigration/immigrants	12%
Crime/law & order/violence/vandalism/anti-social behaviour	11%
Unemployment/factory closure/lack of industry	10%
Defence/foreign affairs/international terrorism	3%
National Health Service/hospitals/healthcare	2%
Education/schools	2%
Drug abuse	2%
Morality/individual behaviour	2%
Inflation/prices	2%

Source: UK Border Agency Public Attitudes Survey, Ipsos MORI. Results are based on 1,040 face-to-face interviews with adults aged 16+ years between 7 August and 7 September 2009.

That doesn't mean that terrorism always achieves its aims, however. 'With political violence for its own sake, or where the terrorist's political demands are non-negotiable and requiring fundamental change of its adversary – then I think it can't achieve its ends,' Professor Taylor believes.

Identifying the next wave

Extreme Islamic-based terrorism will continue, however, and its incidence is likely to rise in the medium term, Professor Taylor predicts. But global jihad will not always be the biggest threat to security, he predicts.

'Environmental concerns, associated with resource allocation and inequalities, movement of people, etc. are a much greater long-term concern, I believe.

'Right-wing terrorism, as a response to current terrorist threats associated with Islam, and also as a response to social changes caused by environmental issues, is another possible development,' he warns.

Professor Taylor is worried that not enough is being done to assess and understand these potential new threats. 'We need to engage more with civil society and business to draw together a coherent collective response,' he stresses. 'The effective management of terrorism cannot continue to be seen as just the job of the State and its organs. We need to develop a more collective approach as we do in other areas like crime prevention.'

Emphasis on risk experts' role

Risk professionals in Lloyd's not only provide insurance for assets and investments in over 150 countries specifically against political violence. They also represent an important resource through their accumulated experience and analysis of events around the world.

Society can be made more resilient to political violence, Professor Taylor believes. 'In my view the insurance industry has a particularly major role to play here, in terms of contributing to our thinking on risk and risk assessment,' he says. 'I firmly believe in the role of education – for professionals and for the public more generally. An educated public will still be hurt and damaged, but better understanding [of the risks] can help to attenuate these effects.'

25 February 2011

⇨ The above information is reprinted with kind permission from Lloyd's. Visit their website at www.lloyds.com for more information on this and other related topics.

© Lloyd's

LLOYD'S

7/7: five years on

Information from YouGov.

By Alex Hourdakis

Five years on from the 7 July 2005 terrorist attack on the London Underground, known as '7/7', more than half (53%) of the UK's population think that the threat of terrorism has stayed at the same level, with older people feeling slightly more worried than their younger counterparts.

However, when we repeated the question in a slightly different way, we see that the public is actually less concerned about terrorism than it thinks – 76% now think future terrorist attacks on British targets are likely, compared to 92% four days after the bombings, which affected three Underground trains and one bus.

Perhaps this general sense of security is due to most (51%) thinking that the last Labour Government dealt with extremism and terrorism 'effectively'. More than a third (35%), however, said that Labour was ineffective in dealing with the threat.

Indeed, a sizeable quarter believes that the threat has actually increased since 2005. Interestingly, women are more likely to think that it has increased (30%) than men (21%). Older people are more worried than their younger counterparts, with 81% of those over 60 believing that future attacks are likely compared to 57% of 18- to 24-year-olds.

As for the public's opinion on how the new Coalition Government is going to fare against terrorism, 41% think that it will be effective, whereas just over a quarter (27%) foresee it being ineffective.

Tube or bus?

The survey also assessed the effect that 7/7 had on people's attitudes to travelling on public transport and found that while most still feel confident, a significant minority remains apprehensive. 58% stated that the attacks did not make them less likely to use public transport; while 22% said it affected them, but only 'for a while'. Only 7% say they are 'still less likely to use public transport'.

Despite these hints of concern, the general feeling among respondents is that any future attacks will be unlikely to affect them personally. When asked about the chances of them or a family member being attacked or wounded as a result of an attack, the majority (59%) felt that the chances were fairly or very low. Nearly a fifth (19%) said the chances were 'almost non-existent'.

Muslims in society

Reassuringly, the bombing, which has been attributed to a group of four British-based Muslims, including Mohammed Sidique Khan, does not seem to have affected the public's perception of Muslims on the whole; the majority (60%) said that it made 'no difference to their opinion'. Perhaps more worryingly, though, a third of respondents quoted that the attacks made them more negative towards British Muslims, and a large 43% of respondents think that since the attacks British Muslims have become 'less integrated' into British society.

7 July 2010

⇨ The above information is reprinted with kind permission from YouGov. Visit www.yougov.com for more.

On the fifth anniversary of the 7/7 London transit attack

Information from the National Consortium for the Study of Terrorism and Responses to Terrorism (START).

July 7 2010 marks the fifth anniversary of the 2005 terrorist attacks on London's metro system. In 2005, terrorists launched a coordinated attack against London's transportation system, with three bombs detonating simultaneously at three different Underground stations and a fourth bomb exploding an hour later on a city bus. In all, there were 52 victims in these bombings with an additional 700 injuries resulting. The four terrorists who executed the attacks were killed in the explosions.

On the fifth anniversary of this deadly attack, START provides this background report to examine the degree to which these attacks reflect changing trends in terrorist activity in Great Britain and globally.

Terrorist attacks in Great Britain

According to START's Global Terrorism Database (GTD), Great Britain (England, Wales and Scotland) has been the target of 604 terrorist attacks since 1970. Great Britain was the sixth most frequent target for terrorists in Western Europe during this period, behind Northern Ireland (3,811 attacks), Spain (3,182), France (2,456), Italy (1,494), Germany (1,095) and Greece (893).

517 of these attacks on Great Britain occurred in the period between 1970 and 1994, while 87 attacks have occurred since 1994 – when the Irish Republican Army declared a ceasefire for the first time in 25 years in the sectarian conflict that had generated thousands of terrorist attacks in Northern Ireland, Great Britain and Ireland since the 1970s. From 1970 to 1994, Great Britain faced an average of 21.5 terrorist attacks per year. From 1995 onwards, Great Britain has been targeted by terrorists in an average of 6.2 attacks per year.

14.6% of all terrorist attacks during this era (1970-2008) were fatal terrorist attacks, resulting in the death of one or more person. The number of annual fatal attacks peaked in 1974 (with 12 fatal attacks) and 1975 (13 fatal attacks). In all, 88 fatal attacks in Great Britain have resulted in the deaths of 553 people – an average of more than six deaths per fatal attack – with the deadliest terrorist attack being the hijacking and destruction of Pan Am Flight 103: as it exploded over Lockerbie, Scotland, it killed 270 people.

Suicide terrorism

One of the distinguishing characteristics of the 7/7 attacks on the London Underground and transportation system was that it was conducted by suicide bombers. This willingness of terrorists in Great Britain to sacrifice their lives in an attack represented a new development. The GTD tracks the usage of suicide techniques by terrorists, and the coordinated bombing in London in 2005 marked the first recorded occurrence of suicide terrorism in Great Britain. Events in subsequent years, however, have demonstrated that suicide terrorism is not the norm in Great Britain: since the 7/7 attacks, there has been only one other attempted suicide attack in Britain – a 2007 attack on Glasgow Airport in which one of the attackers died after suffering burns during the failed attempt.

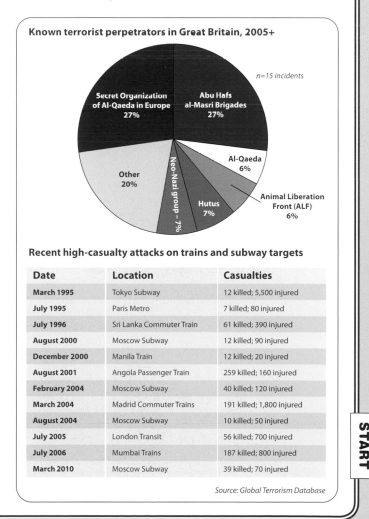

Known terrorist perpetrators in Great Britain, 2005+

n=15 incidents

- Secret Organization of Al-Qaeda in Europe 27%
- Abu Hafs al-Masri Brigades 27%
- Al-Qaeda 6%
- Animal Liberation Front (ALF) 6%
- Hutus 7%
- Neo-Nazi group – 7%
- Other 20%

Recent high-casualty attacks on trains and subway targets

Date	Location	Casualties
March 1995	Tokyo Subway	12 killed; 5,500 injured
July 1995	Paris Metro	7 killed; 80 injured
July 1996	Sri Lanka Commuter Train	61 killed; 390 injured
August 2000	Moscow Subway	12 killed; 90 injured
December 2000	Manila Train	12 killed; 20 injured
August 2001	Angola Passenger Train	259 killed; 160 injured
February 2004	Moscow Subway	40 killed; 120 injured
March 2004	Madrid Commuter Trains	191 killed; 1,800 injured
August 2004	Moscow Subway	10 killed; 50 injured
July 2005	London Transit	56 killed; 700 injured
July 2006	Mumbai Trains	187 killed; 800 injured
March 2010	Moscow Subway	39 killed; 70 injured

Source: Global Terrorism Database

START

The infrequency of suicide attacks in Great Britain does not mean that suicide terrorism rates are holding steady globally. Rather, around the world, suicide terrorism has been on the rise in recent years, with a relatively steady increase starting from 1997 through to 2007. A modest decrease in suicide terrorism is reported for 2008, when 191 such incidents were reported. This frequency of suicide attacks, though, is still well above the average number of suicide attacks per year (1997-2008) of 113 attacks globally. In all, 1,438 suicide terrorist attacks occurred worldwide during this period.

Terrorist perpetrators in Great Britain

Between 1970 and 1999, almost two-thirds of all terrorist attacks in Great Britain with a known perpetrator were the responsibility of the Irish Republican Army or a related Irish nationalist splinter group, responsible for 293 attacks, or 64% of terrorist activity, in Great Britain during this period. While terrorist activity did decline in the late 1990s and 2000s following the Good Friday agreement in Northern Ireland, IRA-related groups were still the main source of British terrorist activity, responsible for 58% of incidents with known perpetrators during this period.

The 7/7 attacks in 2005 represented a departure in terms of the types of perpetrators targeting Great Britain. A previously unknown group called the Secret Organization of al-Qaeda in Europe claimed responsibility for the four coordinated bombings in London on 7 July 2005. In a posting on an Islamic militant website following the attacks, this group indicated that the deadly attacks were launched in retaliation for British involvement in armed conflicts in Iraq and Afghanistan.

Since 2005, Great Britain has experienced attacks from a diverse group of terrorist organisations: in addition to the 7/7 attacks by the Secret Organization of al-Qaeda in Europe, another Jihadist group – Abu Hafs al-Masri Brigades – launched an attack on the London transit system just two weeks after the 7/7 attacks. While this second coordinated attack did not inflict the destruction that the 7/7 attack did, it did create and sustain concerns about Jihadist threats to Great Britain, which has also experienced attacks by animal rights groups and far-right extremists since 2005. In contrast, there were no attacks during this period conducted by Irish nationalists (Irish Republican Army or IRA splinter groups), marking a profound shift from Britain's recent past. This long-time threat has been replaced by a broad array of new threats, including several new groups, willing to take violent action against the British people and Government.

The 7/7 metro attacks are the only known terrorist attack by the Secret Organization of al-Qaeda in Europe, although the group also made unsubstantiated claims of responsibility for terrorist attacks on Madrid commuter trains in March 2004. This emergence of new groups, with no past history of terrorist attacks, is a discernible global trend in this decade. Since 1975, 1,923 organisations have been identified as terrorist perpetrators, each responsible for at least one terrorist attack around the world. From 1975 to 2008, an average of almost 58 new groups emerged per year – groups with no past history of engaging in terrorist attacks – peaking in 1992 with 117 new organisations.

While the mid- to late-1990s saw a decrease in the number of new groups emerging annually (with a low of 19 new groups emerging in 1998), during the last decade the average number of emergent organisations has been on the increase again worldwide, with 41 new organisations emerging annually on average since 2000, and with an increasing number emerging each year since 2004. This trend is similar to peaks evident in the late 1980s – an era of high levels of terrorist activity.

As evidenced by the British example, emergent organisations today do not reflect one ideology, but rather, there are new groups representing a wide array of ideological beliefs and particular goals, complicating counter-terrorism and anti-terrorism efforts in countries around the world.

Coordinated terrorist attacks

Coordinated events involving multiple targets being attacked at the same time and place, like the 7/7 attacks, account for approximately 13% of all attacks worldwide since 1970. These attacks are most often bombings (60%) and are unusual in terms of the degree of organisational sophistication and planning required to carry them out. Coordinated attacks can also pose a unique challenge to responders, creating a strain on resources and a particularly chaotic environment.

Coordinated attacks were fairly rare in the 1970s and early 1980s, making up only 2% to 10% of all attacks. In the mid-1980s this figure doubled, peaking at 30% in 1998. The past ten years have seen a steady decline in the prevalence of coordinated attacks, averaging around 15% of all attacks.

There have been a number of high-profile coordinated attacks in recent years, including the events of 11 September 2001 in the United States, the Bali nightclub bombings in 2002, the commuter train bombings in Madrid in 2004 and the series of armed assaults in Mumbai in November 2008. As suggested by the highly lethal nature of these cases, on average fatal attacks that are part of a coordinated event result in 44% more deaths than fatal attacks that are not part of a coordinated event (averaging 7.8 deaths compared to 5.4 deaths).

START

Terrorists and transportation targets

The 7/7 attacks directly targeted London's transit system, as did the subsequent attack in London two weeks later claimed by Abu Hafs al-Masri Brigades. In addition to these British attacks on transportation targets, recent years have borne witness to terrorist attacks on trains and metro targets in Tokyo, Paris, Sri Lanka, Manila, Angola, Moscow, Madrid and Mumbai. These high-profile, deadly attacks have raised questions about whether transportation infrastructure is especially prone to terrorist activity.

> *Between 1970 and 1999, almost two-thirds of all terrorist attacks in Great Britain with a known perpetrator were the responsibility of the Irish Republican Army or a related Irish nationalist splinter group*

In Great Britain, businesses – not transportation infrastructure – have traditionally been the favoured targets of terrorists, with 38% of British attacks from 1970 through to 2008 directed against private businesses. In contrast, only 7% of terrorist incidents have attacked British transportation targets during this period – a total of 44 such attacks. This rate of attack against British transportation targets is consistent with the global average.

While the rate of such terrorist activity worldwide varies from year to year, it peaked in 1995 and 1996 with attacks on transportation targets representing 8% of the total terrorist activity globally. Worldwide, there was an increase in attacks on transportation targets in 2008, with a jump from 48 such attacks in 2007 to 293 transportation-focused attacks in 2008. However, this still represents only 8% of all terrorist activity in 2008.

Rather than a concentrated focus by terrorist organisations on transportation targets, or any one kind of target, these violent actors continue to attack a wide range of targets. In 2005 – the year of the 7/7 attacks – almost half of all terrorist activity in Great Britain targeted transportation. However, in the previous year (2004), no terrorist attacks in Britain focused on such targets. Rather, almost 80% of attacks targeted businesses. And in 2006, one year after the 7/7 attacks, diplomatic government facilities were the sole target of terrorists in Britain.

This variation in terrorist targeting is no doubt in part a function of terrorists' perception of successful counter-terrorism tactics applied to specific target types – but, in the degree to which shifting targets is a strategy of terrorist organisations, it serves to complicate effective and efficient counter-terrorism measures in Britain and around the world.

Notes on this report

The Global Terrorism Database (GTD, www.start.umd. edu/gtd) contains information on more than 87,000 terrorist incidents that have occurred around the world since 1970. At the time of this report, the GTD covers events from 1970-2008. Additional data from 2008-2010 will be available for download beginning July 2011.

GTD is a project of the National Consortium for the Study of Terrorism and Responses to Terrorism (START), a US Department of Homeland Security Center of Excellence. START, based at the University of Maryland, College Park, aims to provide timely guidance on how to disrupt terrorist networks, reduce the incidence of terrorism, and enhance the resilience of US society in the face of the terrorist threat.

The material presented here is the product of START and does not express the opinions of the US Department of Homeland Security.

For additional information, please contact START at emiller1@start.umd.edu. Questions specifically on the GTD can be directed to gtd@start.umd.edu

⇨ The above information is reprinted with kind permission from the National Consortium for the Study of Terrorism and Responses to Terrorism (START). Visit www.start.umd.edu for more information.

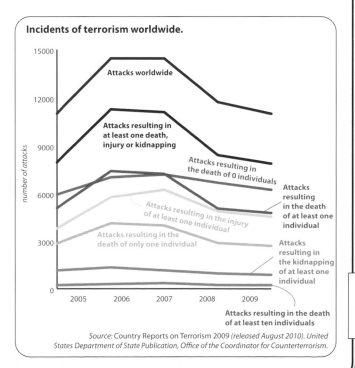

Incidents of terrorism worldwide.

Source: Country Reports on Terrorism 2009 *(released August 2010).* United States Department of State Publication, Office of the Coordinator for Counterterrorism.

Islamist terrorism

The British connections.

Al-Qaeda and al-Qaeda-inspired terrorism remains the biggest threat to the UK's national security. The Security Service estimates that over 2,000 people in the UK pose a terrorist threat and in March 2005 it was estimated that there were up to 200 al-Qaeda-trained operatives in the UK. The British-based threat does not only affect the UK: a number of British Muslims have been convicted in foreign courts or have fought for (or trained with) terrorist or extreme Islamist groups abroad.

Islamist Terrorism: The British Connections aims to present an overview of Islamism-inspired terrorism with significant connections to the UK. The report is a collection of profiles of Islamism-inspired terrorist convictions and attacks in the UK between 1999 and 2009 and a statistical analysis is drawn from the data collected. The report also examines the scope of British-linked, Islamism-inspired terrorism threats worldwide since 1993, including convictions, training and suicide attacks abroad, as well as terrorism extradition cases from the UK. Connections between significant individuals and groups have also been charted.

Significant incidents and precedents

Islamist Terrorism presents significant incidents and precedents, which include the following:

⇨ In 1996 Khalid Shahid is said to have become Britain's first suicide bomber. While fighting jihad in Afghanistan, he asked members of the Taliban to hide grenades in his jacket, which he could detonate when the Northern Alliance tried to arrest him.

⇨ In March 1999 Amer Mirza was the first member of al-Muhajiroun (a group now proscribed in the UK) to be convicted of Islamism-related terrorism offences. He had attempted to petrol bomb a Territorial Army base in West London.

⇨ In January 2002 Moinul Abedin was the first person convicted in UK courts for planning an Islamism-inspired terrorist attack.

⇨ In April 2002 Iftikhar Ali became the first person convicted of inciting racial hatred with an Islamic religious text. Ali was distributing al-Muhajiroun leaflets which called for a holy war against Jews.

⇨ In April 2003 Brahim Benmerzouga and Baghdad Meziane became the first people convicted of funding Islamist-related terrorism through conspiracy to defraud. Al-Qaeda was among those that they had funded.

⇨ In July 2005 Mohammad Sidique Khan, Shehzad Tanweer, Hasib Hussain and Germaine Lindsay became the first suicide bombers to attack the UK.

⇨ In November 2005 Abbas Boutrab was the first person to be convicted of Islamism-related terrorism offences in Northern Ireland.

⇨ In May 2007 Syed Hashmi became the first person to be extradited from the UK to the United States of America on Islamism-related terrorism charges.

⇨ In July 2007 Younes Tsouli was the first person to be convicted of inciting murder for terrorism purposes overseas over the Internet.

⇨ In November 2007 Abdul Rahman became the first person to be convicted of disseminating terrorist information under the Terrorism Act 2006.

⇨ In February 2008 Mohammed al-Figari, Mohammed Hamid, Kader Ahmed, Mohammed Kyriacou, Kibley da Costa, Atilla Ahmet, Yassin Mutegombwa and Mustafa Abdullah were the first people convicted of providing or attending terrorist training in the UK under the Terrorism Act 2006.

⇨ In March 2008 Bilal Mohammed was convicted solely of disseminating terrorist material. This was the first time that section two of the Terrorism Act 2006 had been used independently.

⇨ In April 2008 Simon Keeler became the first British Caucasian Muslim convert to be convicted of Islamism-inspired terrorism charges: he was found guilty of inciting murder for terrorist purposes overseas and fundraising for terrorist purposes.

⇨ In June 2008 Yeshiemebet Girma became the first woman to be convicted of Islamism-related offences. She had assisted one of the conspirators of the failed 21/7 suicide attacks in London in 2005.

⇨ In August 2008 Hammaad Munshi became the youngest British citizen to have been convicted of Islamism-related terrorism offences. Munshi was aged 16 when charged and 18 when convicted.

⇨ In December 2008 Rangzieb Ahmed and Habib Ahmed became the first people in the UK to be convicted of membership of proscribed Islamist organisations. The organisations in this case were al-Qaeda and Harakat ul-Mujahideen.

⇨ In February 2009 Shella Roma became the first woman in Britain to be convicted of distributing terrorist publications.

Statistical analysis

Islamist Terrorism profiles 124 individuals who committed suicide attacks or were convicted for Islamism-related terrorism offences in the UK between 1999 and 2009. There were a combined total of 127 convictions and attacks, which will collectively be referred to as Islamism-related offences (IROs).

Age and gender

Analysis of IROs confirms that Islamism-inspired offences have been most commonly carried out by young men.

⇨ Only five women have been convicted, three of whom were convicted of offences that involved concealing information after an offence and/or assisting an offender rather than violent acts or active participation in a terrorism plot.

⇨ While the age at time of charge ranged from 16 to 48, just over two-thirds of all IROs were committed by those aged under 30. Many of the remaining third were convicted of offences related to their roles as facilitators and/or ideologues.

Education and employment

Analysis of individuals who committed IROs in the UK does not support the assertion made by some that there is a correlation between terrorist activity and low educational achievement and employment status.

⇨ Where known, the most common level of education achieved at the time of the IRO was study for a higher education qualification. Including graduates and postgraduates, therefore, a minimum of 31% of those who committed IROs had at some point attended university or a higher education institute.

⇨ A total of 42% of IROs were perpetrated by individuals either in employment (32%, n=41) or full-time further or higher education (10%, n=13) at the date of charge or attack.

Nationality, origin and place of residence

IRO analysis supports the theory that the UK faces a threat from 'home-grown' terrorism.

⇨ 69% of IROs were perpetrated by individuals holding British nationality.

⇨ South-central Asia features prominently among origins of ancestry, accounting for almost half (46%) of all places of origin by region of ancestry. Furthermore, over a quarter (28%) of those who committed IROs have some Pakistani heritage, of whom at least 80% (n=29) were British nationals with Pakistani origins.

⇨ The most common origin, after British Pakistani (23%) and those of unspecified origins (9%), is Somali, which was the origin of ancestry for eight of those convicted for IROs (6%).

⇨ Among UK residences, London features most prominently, with just under half (48%, n=61) of IROs being committed by individuals living in London. The boroughs of Waltham Forest and Newham within North East London were together home to 30% of London-based perpetrators (n=18). Outside of London, the two most common regions were the West Midlands (13%) and Yorkshire and the Humber (9%).

Charges, sentences, legislation and appeals

Analysis of the 122 IRO convictions (excluding suicide bombers) reveals a spread of severity of charges and length of sentence.

⇨ The most common sentence received for an IRO, given 39 times, was between 13 months and four years (32% of all sentences). Sentences totalling ten years or longer were given 25 times (20% of all sentences) and a life sentence or an indefinite sentence for public protection was given on 23 occasions (19% of all sentences).

⇨ In 44% of IROs, the individual pleaded guilty and in 55% of cases the individual pleaded not guilty.

⇨ 60% of convictions were secured under anti-terrorism legislation, three-quarters of which were under the Terrorism Act 2000.

⇨ Of the 119 individuals convicted of IROs, a minimum of 25 successfully appealed their sentences; three had their sentences increased by the Court of Appeal; and a minimum of 29 were either refused leave to appeal or unsuccessfully appealed their conviction or sentence.

Links to proscribed organisations

⇨ The majority (68%) of individuals who committed IROs had no direct link to any organisations currently proscribed by the UK Government; 40 individuals (32%) did, the two most prevalent being al-Muhajiroun (15%, n=19) and al-Qaeda (14.5%, n=18).

⇨ Just under a third (30%, n=11) of the 37 cell members involved in the eight major terrorism plots had direct links to al-Qaeda, making it disproportionately well represented as an associated organisation among cell members.

⇨ 77.5% (n=31) of those with links to proscribed organisations are British. However, in over half (52.5%, n=21) of all these cases the individual's place of origin of ancestry is in South-central Asia: of these, all of whom are British citizens, 62% (n=13) are British Pakistanis and 19% (n=4) are British Bangladeshis.

Attendance at terrorist training camps

⇨ The majority (69%) of all individuals who committed IROs had not attended terrorist training camps, while just under a third (31%) had attended one or more, the most common location being Pakistan (17%).

⇨ 55% (n=21) of the 38 individuals who attended one or more training camps trained in Pakistan and six of the eight major terrorism cells include members who attended camps there.

⇨ Seven of the eight terrorist cells contained individual members who had attended terrorist training camps and cell members were much more likely to have attended terrorist training camps than all those who were involved in IROs (51% and 31%, respectively).

⇨ The proportion of cell members who trained in Pakistan (38%, n=14) or Afghanistan (11%, n=4) is approximately double that of all individuals involved in IROs (17% and 6%, respectively).

⇨ The majority (68%, n=26) of those who attended terrorist training camps are British.

⇨ Just over half (53%, n=20) of those who attended terrorist training camps are of South-central Asian origin and just under a quarter (24%, n=9) are of East African origin. Of these individuals, the majority (85%, n=17) of those of South-central Asian origin are British citizens, while over half (56%, n=5) of those of East African origin are non-British citizens.

Proscribed organisations and terrorist training

⇨ Half (50%, n=19) of the 38 individuals who attended training camps were linked to one or more proscribed organisations, of which al-Qaeda is the most common (32%, n=12). Just over two-thirds (68%, n=13) of these were also involved in the major terrorism plots.

Al-Qaeda and al-Qaeda inspired terrorism remains the biggest threat to the UK's national security

---

⇨ Two-thirds (68%, n=13) of the 19 individuals who had received terrorist training but were not directly linked to a proscribed organisation were not involved in the major terrorism plots.

⇨ Seven of the eight major cells contained individual members who had direct links to al-Qaeda, of which five involved cell members who had trained in Pakistan: 7/7; the 'fertiliser bomb' cell; the 'dirty bomb' cell; the 'shoe bomb' cell; and the transatlantic 'liquid bomb' cell.

July 2010

⇨ The above information is an extract from the Centre for Social Cohesion's report *Islamist Terrorism: The British Connections*, and is reprinted with permission. Visit www.socialcohesion.co.uk for more information.

© *Robin Simcox, Hannah Stuart & Houriya Ahmed,* Islamist Terrorism: The British Connections *(Centre for Social Cohesion, 2010)*

CENTRE FOR SOCIAL COHESION

Groomed for suicide: how Taliban recruits children for mass murder

Young Afghans being coerced into joining jihad with threats of violence and promises of martyrdom.

By Jon Boone in Kabul

The Taliban gave Noor Mohammad a simple choice – either they would cut off his hand for stealing or he could redeem himself and bring glory on his family by becoming a suicide bomber.

Held in Taliban custody in a different village from his parents, after allegedly stealing mobile phones during a wedding party in his village, the 14-year-old boy went for the second option.

He was soon being given basic lessons in how to use a handgun, which he would use to shoot the guards at a nearby US military base in Ghazni, a province in south-east Afghanistan which is considered the most violent in the country.

He was also fitted with a suicide vest that covered his torso with explosives. He was told that when inside the base he should touch two trailing wires together, killing himself and as many US and Afghan soldiers as possible.

Having kitted the soon-to-be martyr out in his jihadi outfit, the insurgents took photos and sent him on his way. Such is one method by which the Taliban recruit a growing number of children used for suicide missions.

A tactic pioneered by al-Qaeda but almost unheard of in Afghanistan until 2005, suicide bombing is becoming more popular with insurgents attempting to meet the massively intensified NATO campaign with their own surge of violence.

In one recent case a 12-year-old boy in Barmal district in Pakitika province, which borders Pakistan, killed four civilians and wounded many more when he detonated a vest full of explosives in a bazaar.

'They are relying more and more on children,' said Nader Nadery, from the country's Independent Human Rights Commission, who thought the Taliban were struggling to recruit enough adults. 'When somebody runs out of one tool they go to use the second one.'

Mohammad, who talked to the *Guardian* on Tuesday at a children's prison in Kabul, is awaiting trial after surrendering to the Americans rather than going through with the attack.

He says he was left by his Taliban handlers to walk the last few miles to the base in Andar district two weeks ago.

Instead he sat down and thought about his predicament. 'It is a sin to kill yourself and to kill others,' he decided. 'So I took off the vest and threw it away.'

Surrendering proved tricky as the guards he had been supposed to kill were slow to raise the alert and he was questioned only after sleeping outside the camp for a night.

He later led the Americans to the village where the Taliban members lived, identifying a house where the Americans recovered weapons and homemade explosives.

Two Taliban from the village were also killed during a shootout after he identified them, Mohammad said. He knows because of this he will never be able to go back to his village and will probably never see his family again.

Not all bombers are coerced. Some are tricked, like a group of four children who were recently arrested after travelling alone across the border from Pakistan into Afghanistan.

Lutfullah Mashal, the spokesman for the National Directorate of Security (NDS), said his spy agency's informants in Peshawar had raised the alarm that the four were on their way.

The boys had confessed during questioning, telling the security forces they believed only American soldiers would die when they detonated their bombs and that they would escape unscathed.

But, speaking on Tuesday, they claimed they were forced into making a confession after being beaten and threatened with rape by police. Their new account is hard to believe, however, and at times contradictory.

According to Fazal Rahman, a tearful nine-year-old made all the more distressed by the loss of two teeth at the dentist, the idea to travel to Afghanistan came from Maulavi Marouf, the mullah in charge of the Spin Jumad madrasa in the town of Khairabad.

They say an 'uncle' in Kabul phoned Marouf asking him to send some physically weak children for a couple of days of manual labour, unloading a delivery of car batteries from lorries.

None of the boys, who are Afghans but have lived in Pakistan all their lives, has an address or phone number for the man. Nor did they think it necessary to tell their parents they were going to Kabul.

THE GUARDIAN

'Our family is very poor,' said Niaz Mohammad, a nine-year-old who said he used to help his father beg. 'When I was promised 50,000 rupees [£360] to go to Afghanistan, I went immediately.'

But they all describe the madrasa as an institution that cultivated in them a hatred for American soldiers in Afghanistan. 'All the time in Friday prayers the maulavi talked about the Americans in Afghanistan and he told us that we should do jihad, especially on Fridays,' he said.

It is feared that hundreds of children may have been radicalised and turned into bombers in what Haneef Atmar, Afghanistan's former interior minister, describes as 'hate madrasas'.

Suicide bombing has also developed a sinister glamour among the youth of the Pakistan's tribal areas. A video in which a group of children enact a suicide bombing was circulated widely in Pakistan in February, sparking public alarm at how jihad appears to have reached the playground.

It also seems to have reached the Kabul juvenile detention centre, where staff are trying to give the mix of criminals and would-be jihadists a proper education. 'When I told my cellmates I refused to do a suicide attack, none of them could understand why I didn't do it,' said Mohammad.

17 May 2011

Half of secondary heads seek police help on violent extremism

Government-commissioned research reveals extent of school leaders' concerns.

By Kerra Maddern

Almost half of all secondary school headteachers have contacted the police for advice on combating violent extremism, according to new Government-commissioned research.

A quarter of primary heads have asked officers for help, with this figure rising to one in three among those working in London, according to the Ipsos MORI survey of 804 schools.

Department for Education (DfE) officials ordered the study to find out if schools are obeying the new duty to promote community cohesion. Researchers were also asked to find out how many schools were engaged in the Home Office's counter-terrorism strategy, Prevent.

According to the study, the police are not the only port of call. Three-quarters of headteachers overall have requested some kind of help to prevent violent extremism among their pupils.

Other widely-used sources of information are DfE guidance (48 per cent of schools), local authority guidance (32 per cent) and the media (30 per cent).

Heads in richer areas, and those whose pupils come from less multicultural backgrounds, were less likely to have asked for guidance on how to prevent violent extremism.

'It may be that a more detailed understanding of their role in preventing violent extremism is driving secondary schools to seek information and support for their work,' the report says.

'They may also have a more developed sense of the types of support they should be seeking and, in turn, where they might source it.'

Joan McVittie, head of Woodside High School in north London and vice-president of the Association of School and College Leaders, said: 'Heads are asking for information because they want to know what to look out for, and they know they should be alert to potential problems.

A total of 84 per cent of school leaders said they knew 'at least something' about their role in preventing violent extremism

'When I took over the running of this school there was conflict between Turkish and Somalian pupils and we did a huge amount of work to stop this. Now, whatever prejudices pupils have, they dump them at the school gate and we have a good school community.'

The aim of Prevent, which is being reviewed by the Coalition Government, is to stop people from becoming or supporting terrorists. Heads have been asked by the Government to identify issues, run training for teachers and 'engage' the community in their work.

A total of 84 per cent of school leaders said they knew 'at least something' about their role in preventing violent extremism, but 20 per cent said they regarded this work as 'unimportant'.

11 March 2011

⇨ Information from TES Connect. Visit www.tes.co.uk for more.

Animal rights extremists 'more of a problem than Islamists'

Universities have more of a problem with animal rights extremists than Islamist radicals, according to an official report that has been criticised for failing to recognise the depth of the problem.

By Duncan Gardham, Security Correspondent

Universities UK, which represents vice-chancellors, said there was very little that it could do about extremism on campus and instead issued new guidance on the importance of freedom of speech.

But James Brandon, of the counter-extremism think-tank Quilliam, said the report failed to show an understanding or awareness of the speakers who are coming onto university campuses.

'This report sadly appears more concerned with protecting the rights of extremist preachers than with protecting students from radicalisation,' he added.

Lord Carlile, who is overseeing the review of the Prevent strategy to counter violent extremism, said the report showed a 'total failure' to deal with how to identify and handle individuals who might be suspected of radicalising or being radicalised whilst within the university.

He added: 'It's non-optional. The universities have to get over their reluctance to be prepared to look at the issue of radicalisation.'

The report was prompted by the Detroit bomber, a former student at University College London, who tried to blow himself up on an aircraft on Christmas Day 2009 using a device in his underpants.

Umar Farouq Abdulmutallab was only one in a long line of university students who have become involved in terrorism including the fertiliser bomb plot, 7 July and the trans-Atlantic airlines plot.

A recent survey found that 31 per cent of those convicted of terrorist-related offences had attended university and ten per cent were still students when they were arrested.

Think tanks have highlighted a succession of extremist speakers invited to deliver lectures unopposed at university Islamic societies, including UCL.

Professor Malcolm Grant, provost of University College London, who chaired the working group that produced the report, said that universities needed to 'ensure that potentially aberrant behaviour is challenged and communicated to the police where appropriate' but added that 'it is emphatically not their function to impede the exercise of fundamental freedoms, in particular freedom of speech, through additional censorship, surveillance or invasion of privacy.'

The report said only a small number of terrorist cases have involved students or graduates from British universities.

It added that: 'Despite some media reports, the view of experts within government is that the higher education sector does not currently have a major problem with violent extremism, though of course that could change in the future.'

The report said that animal rights activism was the most commonly experienced issue on campus, particularly protests, publicity campaigns and attempts to gain access to animal-testing facilities.

Other problems involved political and religious disagreements – often triggered by events in the Middle East – protests about business and industry, equality rights, and the use of the Welsh language.

Half of universities surveyed said they had experienced challenges in relation to speakers invited to the university, but none of those quoted mentioned Islamist extremists.

The report said: 'Generally there is no easy way to identify those who may move into violent extremism compared to those who may hold extreme views.

'Indeed, the process of radicalisation that may result in violent extremism is normally undertaken in a comparatively private and hidden way.

'Further, it has to be recognised that universities are only one part of the lives of staff and students and that there are other influences on their behaviour and actions.'

The report said that the 'challenges' relating to international politics, animal rights and religion were 'influenced as much by external political or geopolitical events as anything inherent to the universities themselves'.

One university reported that police Special Branch had 'no idea how to communicate' and had 'all sorts of strange ideas about what and how people will report

THE TELEGRAPH

what they think of as suspicious, but which are far from abnormal in a university'.

The Government is currently reviewing how it deals with extremism on campus but a Government source told the *Daily Telegraph*: 'We agree that there is not a major or systemic problem; however, there is evidence of extremist activity on campus and when it happens, the consequences can be extremely serious.'

18 February 2011

© *Telegraph Media Group Limited 2011*

Irish Republican terrorist groups

Several Irish Republican terrorist groups in Northern Ireland reject the 1998 Belfast Agreement and continue to carry out terrorist attacks. These groups were formed after splits within the Provisional IRA (PIRA). They oppose political engagement with the British and Irish Governments on any subject other than the establishment of a united Irish republic.

The two main Republican terrorist groups are the Continuity IRA (CIRA) and the Real IRA (RIRA). The name Óglaigh na hÉireann (ONH – 'soldiers of Ireland' in Irish Gaelic) is also used by Republican terrorist groups.

CIRA and RIRA were established after hardline Provisional IRA members rejected their leadership's decision to engage with the British and Irish Governments. The two breakaway groups consider themselves to be the legitimate successors of the original Irish Republican Army. This view is rejected by mainstream Irish Republicans, who have been strongly critical of both groups.

As Jonathan Evans, the Director General of the Security Service, noted in his September 2010 speech 'The Threat to National Security', the separate identities of these groups are 'based on marginal distinctions and personal rivalries'. It had been thought a few years ago that the threat from terrorism in Northern Ireland would decline as time went on. However, this has not proved to be the case. There has been an ongoing rise in the activity and ambitions of Northern Ireland's Republican terrorist groups over the last few years.

There have been increasing signs of coordination and cooperation between Republican terrorist groups. However, their position is very different to that of the Provisional IRA during the Troubles. PIRA at its height had significant political support in Northern Ireland and had a credible political strategy to operate alongside its terrorist campaign. By contrast, there is little evidence that today's Republican terrorist groups have a viable political programme.

The Independent Monitoring Commission reported in November 2010 that Republican terrorist groups continued to pose a substantial and potentially lethal threat. The groups continue to carry out attacks on the security forces in Northern Ireland, especially the Police Service of Northern Ireland (PSNI).

Their favoured approach is to use improvised explosive devices and firearms. Their attacks have caused a number of deaths and serious injuries over the years. They also continue to engage in so-called 'civil administration' actions within their own communities. This includes activities such as punishment beatings and shootings of people whom they regard as 'anti-social'.

Security forces on both sides of the Irish border are working together to tackle the threat from Republican terrorist groups

RIRA was responsible for the last terrorist campaign in Great Britain in 2000-01. It carried out several attacks in southern England, including a rocket-propelled grenade attack on the Secret Intelligence Service (SIS) building in Vauxhall in September 2000. It carried out car bomb attacks on the BBC Television Centre in London's White City in March 2001 and on Ealing Broadway in August 2001. There was also an unsuccessful attack in Birmingham city centre in November 2001. Five RIRA members were subsequently convicted in connection with the attacks.

Security forces on both sides of the Irish border are working together to tackle the threat from Republican terrorist groups. A number of RIRA and CIRA members have been brought to trial and convicted of a variety of terrorist offences in both the UK and the Republic of Ireland.

⇨ The above information is reprinted with kind permission from MI5. Visit www.mi5.gov.uk for more information.

© *Crown copyright*

Anti-terrorism powers

The Terrorism Act 2000 (TA 2000) and the Anti-Terrorism Crime and Security Act 2001 (ATSA 2001) have widened police powers in recent years with respect to terrorism. There are three published codes of practice under the legislation and the Codes of Practice accompanying PACE have been amended to deal with some of the legislative effects.

The most useful and possibly the only up-to-date source of information on these is to be found on the Home Office website: www.homeoffice.gov.uk

The powers described below are in addition to all the general powers the police have under other legislation: that is, PACE and the common law. They have extra powers at ports and airports that are not included below. This section outlines powers in relation to individuals rather than organisations.

These additional powers apply in the investigation of 'terrorism'. Terrorism is defined by the TA 2000 as follows:

The use or threat of action where the action:

⇨ Involves serious violence against a person;

⇨ Involves serious damage to property;

⇨ Endangers a person's life, other than that of the person committing the action;

⇨ Creates a serious risk to the health or safety of the public or a section of the public; or is designed to seriously interfere with or seriously disrupt an electronic system; and

⇨ The use or threat of this action is designed to influence the Government or to intimidate the public or a section of the public; and

⇨ The use or threat is made for the purpose of advancing a political, religious or ideological cause.

The use or threat of action, as above, which is not intended to influence the government or to intimidate the public or a section of the public will still be terrorism if it involves the use of firearms or explosives.

The term 'action' includes action outside the UK. 'Public' includes the public of any country other than the UK and 'Government' means the Government of the UK or part of the UK or anywhere else.

Proscribed organisations

The Secretary of State has discretion to designate an organisation as a proscribed one, just as (s)he can de-proscribe one. You can find a list of proscribed organisations in Schedule 2 to the TA 2000. The list is updated as necessary. Currently it includes Northern Ireland-related organisations and many others of which the following are just examples:

⇨ Al Qaeda;

⇨ Egyptian Islamic Jihad;

⇨ Al Gama'at al-Islamiya;

⇨ International Sikh Youth Foundation;

⇨ Hisballah External Security Organisation;

LIBERTY

⇨ Kurdistan Workers' Party;

⇨ Palestinian Islamic Jihad-Shaqaqi.

Terrorism offences

Most actions that are usually described as terrorism – such as murder, arson, bombings, etc. – are offences under the general criminal law. However, there are some offences created specifically by the TA 2000. These include:

⇨ Membership of a proscribed organisation or supporting a proscribed organisation.

⇨ Possession of money with intent to use it for terrorism.

⇨ Failure to stop a vehicle in accordance with police requirements under the terrorism legislation.

⇨ Providing instruction or training for the purposes of committing terrorist offences.

Stop and search

[NOTE: THIS SUB-SECTION ONLY WAS UPDATED ON 8 JULY 2011]

The TA 2000 gives the police powers to stop and search both people and vehicles.

If a police officer reasonably suspects that you are a terrorist you can be stopped and searched to discover whether you have anything in your possession that may be evidence that you are a terrorist.

The police can also stop and search people and vehicles (and the people in them) without any grounds to suspect that they are involved in terrorism if an authorisation is in place permitting such searches in that particular location. Such an authorisation (under section 47A of the TA 2000) can only be given by a senior police officer. He/she has to reasonably suspect that an act of terrorism will take place and consider that the authorisation is necessary to prevent it. The area covered by the authorisation and its duration should be no greater than the officer considers necessary. The authorisation can only last for a maximum of 14 days. It will also cease to have effect after 48 hours if it is not confirmed by the Home Secretary within that time.

Searches under a section 47A authorisation have to be carried out by police officers in uniform. The purpose of a search of a person can only be to establish whether that person is someone who is involved in terrorism. Vehicles can only be searched for evidence that it is being used for terrorist purposes. A person being searched can only be required to remove their headgear, footwear, coat, jacket or gloves. Someone who has been searched, or the driver of a vehicle that has been searched, can ask the police to provide written confirmation that the search has taken place.

(NB the search power under section 47A TA 2000 replaces a much wider power under section 44 of the same Act. The Government repealed section 44 [by means of a remedial order under section 10 of the Human Rights Act] in response to the ruling of the European Court of Human Rights in the case of Gillan v the United Kingdom, which held that the search power under section 44 was incompatible with Article 8 of the European Convention. Section 47A will itself cease to have effect when Parliament passes similar provisions in the Protection of Freedoms Bill.)

Powers of arrest

Offences under the terrorism legislation are all arrestable offences and there are also specific powers of arrest in the terrorism legislation. You can be arrested without warrant if you are reasonably suspected of being a terrorist. Because of the wide definition of terrorism it may be possible that you could be arrested under the terrorism legislation or other legislation – or even common law – but if you are arrested under the terrorism legislation the other provisions in relation to investigating terrorism come into operation. This arrest power may well be incompatible with Article 5 of the European Convention.

Search of premises

Police powers to enter and search premises without a warrant generally are wide enough to cover most terrorist situations. Nevertheless there are special powers in the terrorism legislation. A senior police officer can authorise a search of your premises if there are reasonable grounds for believing the case is one of great emergency and that in the interests of the state immediate action is necessary.

There are also powers for the police to cordon off certain areas so that they can enter and search premises within the cordon for material that would be of substantial value to the investigation.

The police may also obtain a warrant from a magistrate to search for material likely to be of substantial value to the investigation, provided that there are reasonable grounds for believing it is on particular premises.

Detention

The legislation permits terrorist suspects to be detained for longer than other suspects and for them to have fewer or more constrained rights. The maximum period of detention without charge for someone arrested under terrorism legislation is 14 days but this is subject to judicial authorisation. Access to a solicitor, although the latter can be consulted privately, can be delayed for 48 hours, with additional grounds for delay to those that apply to other suspects. The same applies to the right to have someone notified of arrest.

⇨ The above information is reprinted with kind permission from Liberty. Visit www.yourrights.org.uk for more.

© Liberty

Should Britain work with 'extremists' to prevent terrorism?

Where do we draw the line?

By Jamie Bartlett and Carl Miller

> ### About the authors
> Jamie Bartlett is head of the independence programme at the think tank Demos.

Very shortly the Government will release its review of 'Prevent'. This is the controversial strand of Britain's counter-terrorism strategy that aims to stop terrorism before it occurs. Prevent is based on the idea that Muslim communities themselves can be very effective in helping 'stem the tide' of potential recruits, by confronting and challenging extremism, building resilience to al-Qaeda's message among young Muslims, and working with local authorities or police when they see signs of such violent radicalisation.

Since 2005, this type of work has been central to the UK's CONTEST counter-terrorism strategy, and in 2008/09 as much as £140m was spent on it. Although

it has been much criticised and perhaps maligned for both its philosophy and its implementation, the Coalition is committed to continuing Prevent.

However, the review has been delayed – it is now three months late – because inside the Government there is disagreement about whom within the Muslim community they should work with to carry it forward. David Cameron's and Nick Clegg's quite different speeches on extremism illustrate this tension. It is not unique to them; the Labour Government was also dogged by this problem.

Simply put, some groups or individuals that hold illiberal, even harmful views, can deliver benefits to Prevent. These are the so-called 'non-violent extremists'. They can sometimes be good at identifying and working with individuals that are vulnerable to terrorist recruitment, and they are sometimes an important source of information. Not always of course. But when it comes to stopping terrorism, 'sometimes' is incredibly important. The effectiveness of such groups is because they are awkward bedfellows for liberals. And yet by funding, or working with, such groups, taxpayers' money may, in effect, subsidise and even legitimise groups that hold views which the Government may rightly believe have no place in British society, even if they are free to hold them.

David Cameron's Munich multiculturalism speech hinted at the Coalition's take on this dilemma. He renounced the Labour experiment of working with 'non-violent extremists', and he pledged that taxpayers' money would not be spent on groups that expound radical or extreme views: those that are anti-democratic, anti-human rights and anti-integration. The day after Cameron's speech it was leaked that the Coalition has cut funding for the controversial but effective counter-extremism STREET project, run by a well-known conservative Salafi, Abdul Haqq-Baker.

There are a number of problems once you accept the premise that public money should be spent on this kind of anti-terrorism strategy. I'm just going to focus on two related ones. First, who should the Government now consider as beyond the pale? Second, how will we know?

From Cameron's speech, it appears 'extremists' will now be off limits. But as anyone who has studied the subject knows, that word is heavily loaded, and difficult to define in a workable way. The aim of Prevent is to directly contribute to national security. Its decisions must surely be based on what any partnership is trying to achieve, and this will need to be informed by tactical policing decisions, not political grandstanding. The

OPENDEMOCRACY

police will sometimes need to work with non-violent extremists if they think it can help achieve public safety – especially if they are providing valuable information. The Brixton Salafis who ran the STREET project I have just mentioned have been fighting Jihadists for years – long before 9/11 – and with considerable success. Cutting funding to effective projects like theirs because of their ideology could be self-defeating. But how does the Government work with successful projects like the STREET initiative, without this involvement extending to tacit or explicit support of the ideologies of the groups involved?

Beyond this, where Prevent work is more about the long-term resilience of communities, the Coalition should draw up some clear, relatively minimal, rules of engagement. I am not going to propose a detailed version. But a line should be drawn at groups that oppose or undermine the democratic and human rights of British citizens, even if they are using perfectly peaceful, liberal means to achieve it. (That is not to say that such groups should be banned but that the Government ought not to fund nor partner with such groups as a matter of general principle.)

This sort of minimal cut-off point – rather than something indefinable like 'extremism' – aims to ensure the public does not financially support ideologies that deny everyone's right to peacefully, constitutionally and democratically pursue their own beliefs. And although Prevent will still be primarily focused on al-Qaeda-inspired terrorism (purely based on the size and extent of the threat), this approach would be equally applicable to other groups.

In respect of the second question, a sound method on which to identify who falls inside these lines is needed. Since 2005, Prevent spending has played out in very public arguments between think-tankers, journalists and politicians. Sections of the media dig up an excerpt from a speech of a leader or member of a group, and hold it aloft as proof of extremist views. Denial follows counter-claim, but like the curate's egg, even the accusation of extremism, rather than any carefully considered evidence, has been enough to force government U-turns. This is not a satisfactory way of dealing with issues of such importance: where political pressure leans on tactical decisions of national security. In this new counter-revolutionary fervour of 'muscular liberalism', there is a danger that this pressure will worsen.

Instead, decisions about whether or not to form a partnership should be based on carefully considering a group's ideology and actions holistically rather than through the selective and politically-motivated presentation of fragmented scraps. The relative importance of governing documents, official statements, websites, speeches and pronouncements must be carefully weighed. These statements must be understood in the context of many others, including those that deny, contradict, nuance and explain. The pronouncement of a dissenting firebrand should be distinguished from an undisputed leader. Painting an accurate picture of a group – which often consists of many shades of grey – is a complex task. I am not saying it will be easy. I am saying that there has to be a balanced and rigorous assessment of groups that are to be publicly supported.

Finally, the Coalition must always leave the door open for groups to reform. Liberals believe that people and groups can and do change over time. Yesterday's extremist is sometimes today's elected representative. Public money can be a useful lever. Having a clear set of criteria and a consistent procedure could serve to strengthen internal voices for reform in extremist groups and bolster support for constitutionalism, democracy and human rights, without forcing it down people's throats.

Counter-terrorism work is only one of the ways in which the Government engages with Muslim groups. I have argued elsewhere that it should not be the primary one. In fact, there is a strong case to scale back Prevent considerably, and invest more resources into dealing with the social and economic difficulties that many Muslim communities face, which have nothing to do with terrorism or extremism at all.

Simply put, some groups or individuals that hold illiberal, even harmful views, can deliver benefits to Prevent. These are the so-called 'non-violent extremists'

However, some form of Prevent will remain. Given this, central and local governments will face an awkward dilemma: that trying to stop violent radicalisation might sometimes mean funding or working with groups that others think are part of the problem. As we have argued above, much depends on the purpose of an intervention. A clear definition about which groups are beyond the pale will help, but this should be consistent with a wider set of liberal values that protect civil and political rights, as well as the liberal system as a whole. It must also allow for the (very liberal) world-view that groups and people can change. This means overcoming the vapours of the London press, not surrendering to them.

16 March 2011

⇨ The above information is reprinted with kind permission from openDemocracy. Visit www.opendemocracy.net for more information.

OPENDEMOCRACY

The Terrorism Acts – the facts

Information from SACC.

The Terrorism Act 2000

The Terrorism Act 2000 greatly widens the definition of terrorism and gives the Government the power to proscribe particular organisations. It criminalises a wide variety of activities considered to be in support of proscribed organisations. It extends UK law to cover activities carried out in foreign countries.

Subsequent terrorism acts have had the effect of introducing changes to the Terrorism Act 2000. Unfortunately, the Government hasn't published a straightforward text of the Act as it now applies, although there have been suggestions that it should do so.

21 groups were proscribed under the Act in March 2001. A further four were proscribed in October 2002 and a following 15 groups were proscribed on 14 October 2005. 46 organisations are currently proscribed, two of them under powers introduced in the Terrorism Act 2006, as glorifying terrorism. A further 14 organisations in Northern Ireland are proscribed under previous legislation.

The Anti-terrorism Crime and Security Act 2001

The key provision of the Anti-terrorism Crime and Security Act 2001 (ATCSA 2001) was section 23 – detention without trial of foreigners who are suspected of terrorism and who could not be deported. This provision was ruled unlawful by the Law Lords in a landmark decision in December 2004 and was allowed to lapse in March 2005 (when it was due for renewal).

The Act also gives the police wide new powers to investigate anyone suspected of activities criminalised by the Terrorism Act 2000.

The Prevention of Terrorism Act 2005

The Act was rushed through Parliament after the detention powers contained in the Anti-terrorism Crime and Security Act 2001 were ruled unlawful by the Law Lords in December 2004. The new Act creates a system of 'control orders' through which the Home Secretary can impose restrictions – including house arrest – on anyone she suspects of a connection with terrorism. Unlike the ATCSA 2001 detention powers, the new powers apply to British citizens as well as to foreign nationals.

Terrorism Act 2006

The Act creates a new offence of 'encouragement' of terrorism and extends the time for which police can hold a terror suspect before making a charge to 28 days. It also introduces a number of other new measures and amendments to existing legislation.

The Counter Terrorism Act 2008

This Act extends the injustice of earlier legislation in a number of ways, including:

⇨ Post-charge questioning of 'terror suspects' – 'terror suspects' can be subjected to further questioning after a criminal charge, even up to the trial date. Saying nothing can count against them at trial.

⇨ 'Terrorist connection' would carry a heavier sentence. Judges can give people longer sentences for ordinary offences if they have a 'terrorism connection' – for example, allegedly supporting a banned 'terrorist' organisation. Such allegations could be based on the broad definition in the Terrorism Act 2000, including normal political activities.

⇨ Freezing of bank accounts – any individual suspected of a terrorist connection can have his bank account frozen by the Treasury.

⇨ Extra punishment without trial beyond the original sentence – convicted 'terrorists' could face a ban on foreign travel once released from jail. They can also be required to tell the police where they go whenever they sleep away from home, in some cases for life.

⇨ New offence for volunteers of not giving information to police – volunteer workers, for example in a youth project or a charity, could be prosecuted for not telling police about suspected 'terrorist' activities. People may be afraid of working for causes such as Palestine in case normal activism strays into 'terrorism'.

⇨ New offence of providing information about the Armed Forces. It becomes an offence to seek or communicate information about the Armed Forces which could be useful to terrorism. This could apply simply to peace protestors telling each other what happens at a military base.

Government plans to use the Act to extend pre-trial detention to 42 days were dropped after a lengthy parliamentary battle.

⇨ The above information is reprinted with kind permission from Scotland Against Criminalising Communities (SACC). Visit www.sacc.org.uk for more.

© SACC

Terrorism Prevention and Investigation Measures Bill

The Terrorism Prevention and Investigation Measures Bill was introduced into the House of Commons on 23 May 2011.

On 26 January 2011 the Home Secretary announced the outcome of the review of counter-terrorism and security powers, including the review of control orders. This included a commitment to repeal control orders and replace them with a more focussed and less intrusive system of terrorism prevention and investigation measures.

The new system will protect the public from individuals who pose a real terrorist threat, but whom we cannot prosecute or, in the case of foreign nationals, deport.

The Terrorism Prevention and Investigation Measures Bill marks a key milestone in the Government's programme to rebalance intrusive security powers and increase safeguards for civil liberties.

> **The new system will protect the public from individuals who pose a real terrorist threat, but whom we cannot prosecute or, in the case of foreign nationals, deport**

The Bill and explanatory notes can be found on the Parliament website (www.parliament.uk).

What will the Terrorism Prevention and Investigation Measures Bill do?

The Bill includes the following provisions:

⇨ repeal of control orders (Prevention of Terrorism Act 2005);

⇨ introduction of replacement system of terrorism prevention and investigation measures;

⇨ increased safeguards for the civil liberties of individuals subject to the measures, including:

  ↳ higher test for the measures to be imposed than exists for control orders;

  ↳ maximum time limit of two years – further measures can only then be imposed if the person has re-engaged in terrorism;

⇨ restrictions that impact on an individual's ability to follow a normal pattern of daily life will be kept to the minimum necessary to protect the public, and will be proportionate and clearly justified. It will be much clearer what restrictions can and cannot be imposed, including:

  ↳ lengthy curfews will be replaced by a more flexible overnight residence requirement;

  ↳ relocation to another part of the country without consent will be scrapped;

  ↳ geographical boundaries will be replaced with the more limited power to impose tightly-defined exclusions from particular areas;

  ↳ individuals subject to the measures must be permitted a landline and a mobile telephone, and a computer with Internet connection;

⇨ broad judicial oversight of the system:

  ↳ high court permission will be needed to impose the measures (or to immediately confirm measures imposed in urgent cases);

  ↳ there will be a full automatic review of each case in which measures will be imposed;

  ↳ rights of appeal for the individual against refusal of a request to revoke or vary the measures;

⇨ a duty on the Secretary of State to consult on the prospects of prosecuting an individual before measures may be imposed, and a duty to keep the necessity of the measures under review while they are in force;

⇨ the independent reviewer of terrorism legislation will publish an annual review of the operation of the system.

The Bill is expected to receive Royal Assent by the end of 2011.

⇨ The above information is reprinted with kind permission from the Home Office. Visit www.homeoffice.gov.uk for more information on this and other related topics.

The counter-terrorism review

Trading liberty for security.

By Dr Michael Lister and Dr Lee Jarvis

About the authors

Michael Lister is Senior Lecturer in Politics at Oxford Brookes University and co-author of *Citizenship in Contemporary Europe* (Edinburgh University Press, 2008).

Lee Jarvis is Lecturer in Politics and International Relations at Swansea University and co-author of *Terrorism: A Critical Introduction* (Palgrave, 2011).

The Home Secretary announced her review of the UK's counter-terrorism and security powers on 13 July 2010. Last week, the review's findings and recommendations were published, accompanied by no small measure of rhetorical fanfare over the victory thus secured for civil liberties in the UK.

Throughout the course of this review, we have been engaged in a research project designed to map public views on measures such as Control Orders and pre-charge detention. And, if the review is to address public concerns over these and other powers, our own findings suggest it will largely disappoint. There are some positives; first, the formalisation of the repeal of Section 44 powers pertaining to Stop and Search without suspicion are likely to be welcomed across the British public. Similarly, the reduction of the period of pre-charge detention (a qualified reduction, but an important one nonetheless) also constitutes a move away from a counter-terrorism assemblage described to us as 'draconian', 'incompatible with democracy' and 'totalitarian'.

Yet, there are grounds for serious concerns about the nature and status of the reformed counter-terrorism apparatus that make any pronouncements of proud days for supporters of civil liberties premature at best.

First, what is striking throughout the review is that the overwhelming source of concern about the Coalition Government's inherited counter-terrorism regime is one of operational effectiveness; whether, that is, the measures are useful in the course of their implementation. Now, clearly, whether counter-terrorism powers are effective is a key concern, perhaps even a central one, to their assessment. But this rather narrow criterion cannot be the only concern meriting the revision of such powers. A major issue around the counter-terrorism apparatus is the impact that it has upon Britain in general and certain communities in particular.

In our research we have encountered a remarkably widespread and pervasive belief that counter-terrorism measures are directed and targeted at ethnic minorities in general, and Muslims in particular. As one respondent put it:

'Since when is [a] Polish guy going to get you know [stopped]… [I]t's not going to happen, is it? It's only going to happen if you're Muslim. All of these are designed to control Muslims.'

Importantly, however, it is not only Muslims who feel targeted by these powers, with other ethnic minority groups reporting similar concerns too. Indeed, and worryingly for British democracy, this view of differential treatment leads many individuals to feel detached from the body politic; a detachment that manifests itself in a retreat into political privatism and passivity. This depoliticisation has numerous potential ramifications, even relating to the review's own narrow emphasis on security and the prevention of further terrorist attacks. Ethnic minority communities are less likely to cooperate with security services if they feel that they are under the heavy hand and ever-watchful eye of the state.

This problem with the counter-terrorism apparatus is noted, very briefly, in the review. But nothing further is said or proposed to ameliorate this situation. Therefore, whilst the review aims to enhance the operational effectiveness of the counter-terrorism apparatus, it does nothing to deal with the festering problem that, in certain parts of the UK, government policy is seen to be targeting wide swathes of its own citizens, producing forms of alienation and disengagement which have potentially serious long-term consequences relating to social cohesion, equality and citizenship.

One might argue that as the counter-terrorism apparatus is 're-balanced', such concerns are dealt with. There are two reasons to doubt this.

First, as suggested at the start, despite the concerted media offensive to promote the review as a resurgent liberalism, closer examination of the proposed changes suggests that in some cases, such as the shift from the Control Order regime to Terrorism Prevention and Investigation Measures (TPIMs), the changes are not as marked as might have been the case. Indeed, regarding TPIMs, the person subject to one may still not see all the evidence against them – something which has caused serious concern amongst the wider population.

Similarly, whilst 14 days is less offensive than 28 days, individuals in this country can still be detained for two weeks without being charged. As many respondents in our research noted, re-establishing one's life, career and community standing after 'disappearing' for a number of days (28 or 14) is not a straightforward matter. Again, the difference between the power to stop and search in a designated area where it is 'expedient' for the prevention of terrorism (in Section 44 of the Terrorism Act, which is to be scrapped) and the revised, reserved power to stop and search without suspicion 'in limited circumstances to protect individual sites… where there are reasonable grounds to suspect an act of terrorism will take place' does not constitute a dramatic political movement.

The revised counter-terrorism apparatus continues to enshrine principles that bend and strain procedural fairness. It is still possible to become subject to serious state power without access to evidence or the ability to challenge detention. The concerns articulated by people with whom we spoke were of principle, not of numbers and amounts. The review seems to focus on a quantitative easing of the apparatus, whilst leaving the broad architecture intact. Taken together, we would argue that the review does little or nothing to restore such procedural fairness or to address the sense that some individuals and communities have of being targeted, and the problems this brings about.

And these problems create challenges and issues in terms of security too. As noted, it has been suggested that disaffection may render counter-terrorism efforts counter-productive as communities will not cooperate with the police and security services. But security is not simply a quality that states possess. At present, the language of 'balancing liberty and security' or 'rebalancing' seems to be prominent. Yet, as noted political theorist Jeremy Waldron asks: What is it that we are actually balancing? He concludes that in actuality it is not the liberty of all for the security of all, but something more akin to the security of the majority for the liberties of the minority. This does not provide justice and, for a minority, has a serious and negative impact on their security. In the process this therefore fails also either to ensure or increase security; for the majority or the minority.

One is reminded of the famous maxim often attributed to Benjamin Franklin that 'one who would trade liberty for security deserves neither'. As people we spoke to in our research confirmed, security is often understood by people in terms akin to liberty and freedom. Security and liberty are not viewed as oppositional goods by many people, which need to be traded off or balanced, but rather as elements on the same continuum. To think that some of one can be traded for some of the other seems erroneous, dangerous, unjust and illiberal. To suggest that a review that continues to do so marks a glorious day for civil liberties (or security) is flawed at best, and specious and fatuous at worst.

5 February 2011

⇨ The above information is reprinted with kind permission from openDemocracy. Visit www.opendemocracy.net for more information.

© *openDemocracy*

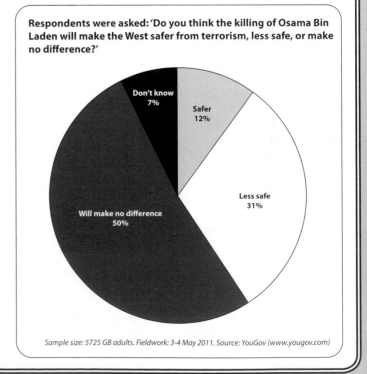

Respondents were asked: 'Do you think the killing of Osama Bin Laden will make the West safer from terrorism, less safe, or make no difference?'

Don't know 7%

Safer 12%

Less safe 31%

Will make no difference 50%

Sample size: 5725 GB adults. Fieldwork: 3-4 May 2011. Source: YouGov (www.yougov.com)

OPENDEMOCRACY

Al-Qaeda will seek revenge

Death of Osama bin Laden not the end of 'war on terror'.

By Julian Borger, Diplomatic Editor

As the US enjoyed its moment of long-delayed catharsis, there was a tantalising sense that a decisive moment might have been reached.

Announcing Osama bin Laden's death, President Barack Obama declared the world a safer place. That could be true in the long term. In the short term, we may be about to find out how much fight al-Qaeda has left.

The US and its allies must brace themselves for reprisals from al-Qaeda cells and affiliates. The suicide blast at a Marrakech cafe and the arrest of three al-Qaeda suspects in Germany last week were a reminder that the organisation's reach is still broad.

Instant suicide attacks may now be unleashed or plots still in the planning pipeline brought forward.

The level of violence could well spike as the disparate groups that carry the al-Qaeda name aim to avenge the killing of their leader. If they fail to do so, their supporters and enemies could rightly question whether they are still a force to be reckoned with.

The struggle against international terrorism, and against al-Qaeda in particular, does not give itself to neat beginnings and endings. The original idea of declaring a 'war on terror' is now widely seen as a mistake. In 2009, the then Foreign Secretary, David Miliband, called for its abolition, saying it united the West's enemies rather than dividing them. Obama agreed and the phrase was quietly banned.

The danger posed by Islamist terrorists remains, but it is now more likely to be treated as a law enforcement and intelligence challenge rather than as an existential threat. Bin Laden's death comes at a time when al-Qaeda's influence is on the wane in the Arab and wider Islamic world.

Al-Qaeda has been conspicuous by its absence in the Arab spring. To most of the revolutionaries in Tunisia, Egypt and Libya, bin Laden was irrelevant. But it is still possible that disillusion, violence and the indecisive NATO intervention in Libya could create opportunities for jihadists.

The continuing challenge will require more co-ordinated international action. Bin Laden's greatest achievement after being driven out of Afghanistan in 2001 was to build an organisation that would survive him. The new al-Qaeda is a loose global network, which in its most diluted form is little more than a franchise that groups around the world can sign up to, exchanging oaths of allegiance for the dread the name inspires.

In the absence of any plausible successor, that loose network is liable to fragment. Ayman al-Zawahiri, the aged, mumbling Egyptian doctor who has fulfilled the role of deputy since 1988, lacks bin Laden's calm charisma.

With the decline of 'al-Qaeda central', subsidiaries will gain ground. Al-Qaeda in the Arabian Peninsula could be an early forerunner. The Yemen-based group showed its ingenuity in November, smuggling bombs inside printer cartridges on to planes flying to the west.

However, al-Qaeda today is less able to mount a spectacular mass-casualty outrage. The organisation has lost bin Laden's grand ambitions and the cohesion necessary to launch a sophisticated attack.

Furthermore, a trove of computer records seized at bin Laden's Abbottabad hideout may help unravel many of al-Qaeda's far-flung networks, and further weaken what the White House terrorism adviser called a 'mortally wounded tiger'.

But while the threat of a devastating attack on the west has receded, the constant menace of the suicide attack in a cafe, or the bomb on a plane, will be with us for some time to come.

2 May 2011

THE GUARDIAN

Victory in the war on terror is now within the West's reach

After Osama bin Laden's death, we can finally destroy al-Qaeda and finish the job in Afghanistan.

By Con Coughlin

Osama bin Laden has only just been consigned to his watery grave in the Arabian Sea, but already politicians on both sides of the Atlantic are debating how best they can exploit any peace dividend from his demise.

In both London and Washington, it is mooted that bin Laden's death will speed up the withdrawal of British and American troops from Afghanistan. In the Commons this week, David Cameron said that his removal raised the possibility of a 'more rapid solution' to the decade-long conflict. In Washington, Republicans and Democrats have both expressed support for an early exit. Barney Frank, a Democratic congressman, put it most succinctly: 'We went there to get Osama bin Laden. And we have now gotten him.'

> **With bin Laden gone, the desire to declare 'mission accomplished' and withdraw our troops from the fray is perfectly understandable. But to do so would be foolhardy in the extreme**

The Republicans, on the other hand, are more concerned about the spiralling cost of America's continued involvement in Afghanistan. (And they should know, after the mind-boggling $1 trillion they ineptly squandered on Iraq.) Current US expenditure there is running at $100 billion a year; even Richard Lugar, the most prominent Republican on the Senate's foreign affairs committee, has questioned whether this represents 'a rational allocation of our military and financial assets'.

It is not difficult to see why an early withdrawal from Afghanistan might appeal to Mr Obama, who has often appeared lukewarm about a conflict that – much to his chagrin – has been dubbed 'Obama's War' since his decision in 2009 to endorse the military 'surge'. Long before he sanctioned the daring special forces mission to terminate bin Laden's gruesome career, the President had spoken publicly of his desire to begin withdrawing US troops later this year. The operation's success will surely stiffen his resolve to follow his political instincts and bring forward the deadline for the cessation of combat operations, which are currently scheduled to last until 2014. What better campaign slogan for next year's presidential contest than 'First we got bin Laden, and then we got the hell out'?

But hang on a minute. Just because we no longer have to endure bin Laden's rambling anti-Western tirades does not mean that the threat to our security and wellbeing has suddenly evaporated. In Britain, the current threat from terrorism is classed as 'severe', which means our intelligence and security services believe there is a strong likelihood that we will be the target of a major attack in the near future.

In America, too, Mr Obama can count himself lucky that a series of recent plots, from the underpants bomber at Detroit airport to the devices concealed in printer cartridges, were foiled. But, to quote the spooks' favourite mantra, the enemy only needs to get lucky once.

With bin Laden gone, the desire to declare 'mission accomplished' and withdraw our troops from the fray is perfectly understandable. But to do so would be foolhardy in the extreme. For, rather than seeing the al-Qaeda leader's removal from the scene as the final act in the war on terror, it should be seen as a decisive breakthrough – and one that could provide the West with the ability to press home its advantage on a number of fronts, and achieve a comprehensive and lasting victory.

The first priority, of course, must be to eviscerate whatever remains of al-Qaeda's infrastructure, particularly in Pakistan. The past ten years have taken a heavy toll on the organisation, and its ability to conduct 'spectacular' attacks of the 11 September variety. At least half of al-Qaeda's senior commanders have been killed or captured, and the life expectancy of anyone brave enough to become its head of operations averages about six months.

That said, al-Qaeda still retains the ability to mount attacks against the West, both from its long-term base in north Waziristan and through its more recently established franchises in Yemen and Somalia. Precisely how the different strands of the brand interconnect will become a lot clearer once the CIA has had time to decipher the 'mother lode' of material – computers, documents and DVDs – seized during the raid on bin Laden's Abbottabad hideout.

THE TELEGRAPH

The prospects of crippling al-Qaeda's operations in Pakistan will also have increased considerably as a consequence of the Pakistani Government's deep embarrassment that bin Laden was able to hide on its soil for at least six years. If Islamabad is ever to distance itself from Mr Cameron's wounding but apposite accusation that it faces 'both ways' in the fight against terrorism, then it can start by taking effective action to root out the last remnants of al-Qaeda's leadership from territory it is supposed to control.

> *In life, bin Laden proved to be an inspirational figure not just for al-Qaeda recruits, but for an entire generation of young Muslims who were susceptible to the appeal of his uncompromising Islamist agenda*

Removing the organisation from its safe haven in Pakistan would certainly bring benefits to the NATO mission in neighbouring Afghanistan, where American and British troops are engaged in a bitter war against the Taliban, for many years al-Qaeda's allies and protectors. The origins of the current conflict lie in the Taliban's refusal to surrender bin Laden to the Americans following the 11 September attacks. His death will already have raised doubts in the minds of moderate Taliban leaders about the wisdom of pursuing their struggle on behalf of a deceased ally. And the removal of al-Qaeda's surviving leaders would certainly help to create the conditions whereby the Taliban felt it was no longer under an obligation to protect its erstwhile supporters, and might instead focus its attention on negotiating an end to the conflict. If that happened, then we really could start to consider an early exit.

Nor should bin Laden's death, and the defeat of his organisation, be seen solely within the context of the bitter conflict being fought along the Afghan-Pakistani border. In life, bin Laden proved to be an inspirational figure not just for al-Qaeda recruits, but for an entire generation of young Muslims who were susceptible to the appeal of his uncompromising Islamist agenda.

However, the wave of anti-government protests that has swept through the Arab world has thrown up the prospect of a very different set of priorities. One of the reasons radical Islam was said to appeal to many young Muslims was that it presented an escape route from an existence otherwise bereft of opportunity or prosperity. But recent events in Egypt and Tunisia suggest there is a better way – namely, embracing the cause of democracy.

During the anti-government protests of Tunisia's Jasmine Revolution, and the demonstrations in Tahrir Square that led to the overthrow of Hosni Mubarak, it was noticeable that the overwhelming majority of the protesters were secularists who wanted to make a better life for themselves and their families. The same is true of the rebels currently battling to overthrow Colonel Gaddafi in Libya, and those who have attempted to challenge Syria's Bashir al-Assad. They are motivated by a desire for freedom and opportunity, rather than the dictates of the mosque.

Bin Laden's influence was on the wane long before the Navy Seals stormed his hideaway, and the Arab Spring has reinforced the view among many young Muslims that there is a viable alternative to his violent Islamist agenda. His death simply confirms that the pendulum has swung back firmly in the West's favour.

4 May 2011

THE TELEGRAPH

Stop trying to balance liberty with security

Exaggerated fear of terrorism should not be allowed to water down our most fundamental freedoms.

By Tim Black

From the countless amendments and additions to the Counter Terrorism Act to the ever-expanding Regulation of Investigatory Powers Act, there's no doubting that British anti-terrorist legislation since 9/11 now constitutes a mightily oppressive edifice.

Under the powers granted to the state over the past ten years, we can be imprisoned on the basis of so-called inciteful speech, we can be detained without charge for days upon end, we can be held under *de facto* house arrest, we can be stopped and searched at will… on and on the liberty-squeezing measures go. All under the guise of protecting us from the potential terror in our midst.

Last week, however, the state issued what looks like a *mea culpa*. 'I think we saw some powers, some laws, enacted which did go too far.' Coming from Lord MacDonald, the man overseeing the Lib-Con Government's review of counter-terrorism legislation, this is quite an admission. Though the actual reforms to existing legislation are yet to be announced, they are expected to include the curtailment of random stop and searches, the replacement of house-arrest style control orders with a system of monitoring, and no recommendation for the extension of detention without charge beyond its existing 14-day limit.

So, a victory for liberty, right? Well, not quite.

Through all the half-baked support and half-arsed criticism, what has been remarkable about the debate around counter-terrorism legislation is just how cowardly it has been. No one seems capable of mounting a defence of what this draconian morass, this testament to New Labourite authoritarianism, has actually undermined over the past ten years – namely, our liberty. Instead, both sides seem intent on battling over the caveats, on drawing the line that shows where liberty ends and security concerns begin. In the words of the fence-sitting *Economist* magazine, the proposed reforms strike 'a reasonable balance between undoing [the then New Labour Government's] most illiberal measures and the requirements of public safety'.

Over and over again, this same freedom-versus-safety dilemma is repeated: 'It is a sign of a healthy democracy', ran a *Telegraph* editorial, 'that we continue to agonise over the proper balance between civil liberties and their infringement by counter-terrorist laws that no reasonable person wishes to see but which are necessitated by the nature of the threat we face'. Lord MacDonald was similarly equivocal: 'We want to protect our constitution, we need to protect our way of life, and we need to get this balance [between security and liberty] right, and I think that is what the review has been trying to achieve.' Lord Carlile, a fellow reviewer of Britain's anti-terror laws, was keen to point out just how difficult it is to calibrate freedom and protection. 'It's art, not science,' he said. 'This is a vital day for the balance between civil liberties and national security.'

SPIKED

If those charged by the Lib-Cons with reviewing existing legislation were predictably cautious, then those wheeled out to defend liberty fared little better. It's not that they don't want to declare that freedom from the state is a good thing – it's just that, well, there are lots of risks out there. Hence even Cerie Bullivant, someone who endured a control order between 2006 and 2008, was only able to attack existing legislation in terms of the extent to which it threatens our security – that is, by apparently 'feeding into the future radicalisation of young people within our own communities'.

Liberty, it seems, is just too lonely and vulnerable by itself. Everywhere it is advocated, its cloying partner security is dragged along, too. The existential threats are too great and the risks too large for freedom to be defended without adding a qualifying clause about the dangers just waiting in the wings. Even campaign group Liberty feels the need to mention the demands of security, insisting that its activists have 'never been naive to or unconcerned with threats from terrorism'. Liberty vs security: it's the conundrum that bewitches both sides.

Yet to defend liberty properly, to champion freedom loudly, all talk of security must be dropped. Because when security is invoked, as if it is a necessary caveat to our liberty, then it robs liberty of its virtues and attributes. For if liberty means to be at liberty to exercise control over our lives, then security means to be secured from doing precisely that. It means to be secured against our worst selves. That is, given full freedom, the freedom to speak our minds, the freedom to associate with whom

we choose, the freedom to exercise our own moral judgement regarding our lives, we will prove incapable of exercising it wisely apparently. That is why, under the watchful gaze of the state, we the not-to-be-trusted must be secured against our own freedom. Because we just might, given our fecklessness, do something terroristic. The ever-expanding volume of blather about security is really an index of the extent to which the state thinks we are incapable of being free.

What the state too often portrays as a balancing act between two separate and opposing things, freedom and security, really boils down to one single thing: the suspicion of the autonomous individual. This is key. For what has undermined the sense of unadulterated liberty, what has corroded this notion of freedom, is a fear of other people. Or better still, a fear of other people's autonomy, a fear that other people, if left to their own moral devices, will commit an atrocity. Hence the state must be allowed to survey people, to snoop on and search us. Over and over again, this suspicion has eaten into the debate about civil liberties. And until it is ejected, the debate around what the state can and can't do to prevent terrorism will remain a cowardly one.

Tim Black is senior writer at spiked.
1 February 2011

⇨ The above information is reprinted with kind permission from spiked. Visit www.spiked-online.com for more information.

Only one in four terror suspects charged

Information from AsianImage.

nly one in four terror suspects were charged with a terrorism-related offence last year, figures showed.

A total of 130 people were arrested on suspicion of being involved in terrorism in the 12 months to September 2010, but only 36 were charged with a terror-related offence.

Almost one in two were released without charge, the figures published by the Home Office showed.

The number of terror-related arrests also fell 35% compared with 201 in the previous 12 months.

None of the suspects were held in pre-charge detention for more than 14 days and more than three in five were dealt with within 48 hours, the figures showed.

A total of 1,897 terrorism arrests have been made since the 11 September terror attacks in the United States in 2001, with 420 charged with terrorism-related offences and 240 convicted. Of the others, 32 were still awaiting prosecution at the end of December.

The figures also showed that 20 prisoners convicted of terrorism-related offences were released between April and September last year, including four who had served four years or more behind bars.

A further 111 were in prison in Britain for extremism or terror-related offences, with 22 classed as domestic extremists or separatists, on 30 September last year.

24 February 2011

⇨ The above information is reprinted with kind permission from AsianImage. Visit www.asianimage. co.uk for more information.

Stop and search figures 'hide evidence of systematic anti-Muslim discrimination'

Home Office's latest figures on numbers of people stopped and searched under anti-terrorism legislation fail to give the full picture when it comes to Muslim concerns about the discriminatory use of the powers.

Massoud Shadjareh, the Chairman of the Islamic Human Rights Commission, said today that the Home Office's latest figures on numbers of people stopped and searched under anti-terrorism legislation fail to give the full picture when it comes to Muslim concerns about the discriminatory use of the powers to target Muslims in particular.

Shadjareh, who sits on the National Police Authority's Stop and Search Community Panel and the Association of Chief Police Officer's Schedule 7 National Accountability Board, was speaking after the Home Office released figures of arrests, convictions and other outcomes under the anti-terror legislation for year ending May 2010 (see http://rds.homeoffice.gov.uk/rds/stats-release.html).

These included data about the numbers of people stopped under stop and search provisions, which showed that over 101,000 people were stopped under Section 44 of the Terrorism Act without a single arrest for anything terrorism related, and over 85,000 people were stopped under Schedule 7, which governs ports and airports. No outcomes were reported for the latter category.

> **'Unfortunately the figures on stop and search released by the Home Office this morning are very limited in their scope, and fail to address suspicions of systematic Islamophobia and anti-Muslim discrimination'**

Shadjareh said:

'Unfortunately the figures on stop-and-search released by the Home Office this morning are very limited in their scope, and fail to address suspicions of systematic Islamophobia and anti-Muslim discrimination.

'It is very disappointing that these crucial figures about how the security agencies deal with large numbers of people who are totally innocent, and have given no grounds for suspicion, are presented as a minor addendum at the end of a 48-page document giving much more detail about the relatively small number of people actually arrested for or convicted of terrorist-related offences.

'The treatment of nearly 200,000 people arrested under stop and search provisions of different kinds need to be taken much more seriously. Accounts we have received from members of the community who have been stopped under these provisions, and sometimes subjected to quite appalling behaviour, raise serious issues that these figures do not address.

'The failure to provide any detailed breakdowns on figures on Schedule 7 stops, under which people can be held and questioned for up to nine hours and can be imprisoned for up to three months for failure to answer questions, is particularly worrying. The Government must have these figures; the fact that they choose not to disclose them

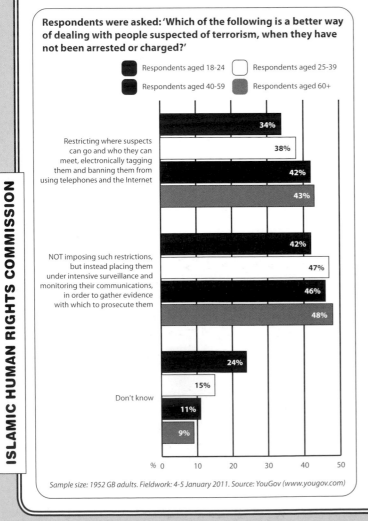

Respondents were asked: 'Which of the following is a better way of dealing with people suspected of terrorism, when they have not been arrested or charged?'

- Respondents aged 18-24
- Respondents aged 25-39
- Respondents aged 40-59
- Respondents aged 60+

Restricting where suspects can go and who they can meet, electronically tagging them and banning them from using telephones and the Internet
- 34%
- 38%
- 42%
- 43%

NOT imposing such restrictions, but instead placing them under intensive surveillance and monitoring their communications, in order to gather evidence with which to prosecute them
- 42%
- 47%
- 46%
- 48%

Don't know
- 24%
- 15%
- 11%
- 9%

Sample size: 1952 GB adults. Fieldwork: 4-5 January 2011. Source: YouGov (www.yougov.com)

ISLAMIC HUMAN RIGHTS COMMISSION

makes it difficult to analyse the effectiveness of the measure, and raises questions about their intentions.

'The reality is that although the total number of people stopped may include members of all communities, it is clear that some ethnic groups are still being disproportionately targeted. Even these figures hide the fact that the numbers of Muslims in particular are still being singled out, not only for searching, but also for more detailed interrogation and being detained for up to the maximum period allowed.

> **'Muslims are also concerned about the attitude of many police officers carrying out the stops, who seem to assume guilt rather than innocence on the part of Muslims, and the sorts of questions that are often asked'**

'Muslims are also concerned about the attitude of many police officers carrying out the stops, who seem to assume guilt rather than innocence on the part of Muslims, and the sorts of questions that are often asked. Security issues do not require people to say what mosques they attend or whether they have ever visited particular countries, for example.

'It is also a matter of concern that fingerprints and DNA are taken from some of those stopped and detained, even though they have been stopped at random rather than on the basis of any supposed grounds for suspicion, and are not even under arrest, let alone charged with anything.

'And it is particularly worrying when, after a long period of detention and questioning that is often perceived as hostile, young people are then asked whether they want to work for the security services as informers in the community. Such questions are often taken as carrying an implied threat as to the consequences should the individual not wish to be recruited in this way.

'In the last few days, we have seen welcome scepticism about unnecessary airport security procedures from Martin Broughton and others in the airline industry. Now we need a similarly sceptical and practical examination of stop-and-search procedures that supposedly form a key element of this country's security provisions, but are clearly shown by these figures to be irrelevant and useless, as well as a waste of money and resources.

'We call on the Government to face up to the real concerns that the increasing disproportionality of stop-and-search is doing nothing to tackle real criminality, but is targeting and criminalising communities that are already suffering alienation and discrimination.'

28 October 2010

⇨ The above information is reprinted with kind permission from the Islamic Human Rights Commission (IHRC). Visit www.ihrc.org.uk for more information.

© Islamic Human Rights Commission (IHRC)

ISLAMIC HUMAN RIGHTS COMMISSION

Searchlight on religion

A major new source of public opinion data on religion and inter-faith relations has just become available in the form of a Populus poll for Searchlight Educational Trust.

By Clive Field, British Religion in Numbers, University of Manchester

The survey is of unusual importance in terms of the number of questions asked and the large size of the sample (5,054 adults aged 18 and over interviewed online in England between 28-31 January 2011).

The Trust is a registered charity formed in 1992 that works with communities to build responses to racism and hatred, dispel myths and develop greater understanding. It has just established the Together project to explore and tackle the rise of right-wing nationalism and extremism in Britain and western Europe.

25% viewed Islam as a dangerous religion which incites violence

Only a small proportion of the poll's statistics have been included in Searchlight's *Fear & HOPE* report, based on the survey, which concluded that 'there is not a progressive majority in society and… that there is a deep resentment to immigration, as well as scepticism towards multiculturalism.

'There is a widespread fear of the "Other", particularly Muslims, and there is an appetite for a new right-wing political party that has none of the fascist trappings of the British National Party or the violence of the English Defence League. With a clear correlation between economic pessimism and negative views to immigration, the situation is likely to get worse over the next few years.'

At the same time, 'there are also many positive findings from the report. Young people are more hopeful about the future and more open to living in an ethnically diverse society. The vast majority… reject political violence and view white anti-Muslim extremists as just as bad as Muslim extremists and there is overwhelming support for a positive campaign against extremism.'

The document is available, in a somewhat curious format, at: http://www.fearandhope.org.uk/project-report/

In this summary, we have drawn upon, but cannot claim to have summarised adequately, the report's numerous tables (128 tables within 395 pages). These provide topline responses, the only ones used here, together with disaggregations by gender, age, socio-economic group, region, employment sector, ethnicity, religion, and a sixfold segmentation by identity 'tribes'. These tables can be accessed at: http://populuslimited.com/uploads/download_pdf-310111-Searchlight-Fear-and-Hope-survey.pdf

Two clusters of questions are briefly considered here, those which sought to enumerate the nation's general verdict on and participation in religion, and those which assessed attitudes to and engagement with people from the various faith traditions in Britain.*

* Only the figures on inter-faith relations are included in this extract.

Inter-faith relations

⇨ 62% considered religious abuse to be as serious as racial abuse, but 38% viewed the latter as more serious (table 115).

⇨ 28% thought religious abuse to be more widespread in Britain than racial abuse. 72% said the reverse (table 116).

⇨ 71% assessed religious abuse to be on the increase in Britain, 29% disagreeing (table 117). 64% said that racial abuse was growing (table 118).

⇨ 60% believed that people should be able to say what they wanted about religion, however critical or offensive it might be. 40% thought there should be restrictions on what individuals could say about religion, and that they should be prosecuted if necessary (table 119). Significantly more, 58%, were in favour of limitations on freedom of speech when it came to race (table 120).

⇨ 44% regarded Muslims as completely different to themselves in terms of habits, customs and values. Just 5% said the same about Christians, 19% about Jews, 28% about Hindus and 29% about Sikhs (tables 78-83).

⇨ 42% said that they interacted with Sikhs less than monthly or never, 39% with Jews, 36% with Hindus, 28% with Muslims and 5% with Christians. There were a lot of don't knows for this question (tables 84-89).

⇨ 59% did not know any Sikhs well as friends and family members, work colleagues, children's friends or neighbours. 55% said the same about Jews, 53% about Hindus, 41% about Muslims and 8% about Christians (tables 90-95).

⇨ 32% argued that Muslims created a lot of problems in the UK. Far fewer said this about other faith groups: 7% about Hindus, 6% about Sikhs, 5% about Christians and 3% about Jews (tables 96-101).

⇨ 49% contended that Muslims created a lot of problems in the world. Again, this was much less often said about other faith communities: 15% about Jews, 12% about Christians, 10% about Hindus and 9% about Sikhs (tables 102-107).

⇨ 25% viewed Islam as a dangerous religion which incites violence. 21% considered that violence or terrorism on the part of some Muslims is unsurprising given the actions of the West in the Muslim world and the hostility towards Muslims in Britain.

⇨ 49% thought that such violence or terrorism was unsurprising on account of the activities and statements of a few Muslim extremists. 6% dismissed accusations of violence or terrorism by Muslims as something got up by the media (table 126).

⇨ On hearing reports of violent clashes between English nationalist extremists and Muslim extremists, 26% would sympathise with the former who were standing up for their country and 6% for the Muslims who were standing up for their faith. 68% would view both groups as just as bad as each other (table 127).

⇨ 43% indicated that they would support a campaign to stop the building of a new mosque in their locality, against 19% who would oppose such a campaign, with 38% neutral (table 124).

⇨ In the event of such a campaign turning violent, or threatening to do so, by the action of either of the disputing parties, 81% would condemn such violence but 19% would continue to support one side or the other (table 125).

⇨ Interviewees were asked to react to the possibility of a new political party which would defend the English, create an English Parliament, control immigration, challenge Islamic extremism, restrict the construction of mosques, and make it compulsory for all public buildings to fly the St George's flag or Union Jack. 21% said that they would definitely support such a party and a further 27% that they would consider backing it (table 122).

⇨ Quizzed about a new organisation which would campaign against religious and racial extremism, and promote better relations between different ethnic and religious groups, 20% said that they would definitely and another 48% that they might possibly support it (table 123).

Hopefully, this gallop through a veritable mountain of statistics will give BRIN readers some insight into the range of questions posed in this Populus/Searchlight survey, and some sense of the research potential of the dataset.

5 March 2011

⇨ The above information is reprinted with kind permission from British Religion in Numbers (BRIN). Visit www.brin.ac.uk for more.

© *University of Manchester*

UNIVERSITY OF MANCHESTER

Misconceptions about Islam and terrorism

Information from Islam is Peace.

Misconception 1: Jihad means holy war

In Arabic, the word 'jihad' means to strive, struggle and exert effort. It is a central and broad Islamic concept that primarily means to struggle against evil inclinations within oneself.

Islam is not confined to the boundaries of the individual but extends to the welfare of society and humanity in general. An individual cannot keep improving himself/herself in isolation from what happens in their community or in the world at large. Hence, it also means to struggle to improve the quality of life in society and the struggle against injustice, oppression and tyranny.

The word 'Jihad' is generally misunderstood and consequently evokes strong reactions. It is a word frequently used in the press, directly or subtly, to mean holy war. In fact the term 'holy war' was coined in Europe during the period of the Crusades. It is an alien concept to the Islamic framework. War is not 'holy'.

Misconception 2: Islamic fundamentalism

In recent years, a great deal of attention in the media has been given to the threat of 'Islamic Fundamentalism'. Unfortunately, due to a twisted mixture of biased reporting in the media and the actions of some misguided

Muslims, the word 'Islam' has become almost synonymous with 'terrorism'. However, when one analyses the situation, the question that should come to mind is: do the teachings of Islam encourage terrorism? The answer: certainly not! Islam totally forbids the terrorist acts that are carried out by some misguided people.

Islam encourages peace, mercy and forgiveness. Killing innocent people totally contradicts the teachings of Islam.

Misconception 3: Terrorism is supported in Islam

This misconception is one of the most widely held misconceptions about Islam today.

The Qur'an states:

'...Whoever kills an innocent soul it is as if he killed the whole of Mankind. And whoever saves one, it is as if he saved the whole of Mankind...' (Surah Al Maidah, Chapter 5 Verse 32)

It is clearly Islamically unlawful to murder an innocent person. Hence, if anyone kills an innocent person, they have committed a grave sin, and certainly the action cannot be claimed to have been done 'in the name of Islam'.

Misconception 4: Islam is intolerant of other religions

The Qur'an states:

'Those who believe in the Qur'an, and those who follow the Jewish (scriptures), and the Christians and the Sabians – any who believe in God and the last day, and work righteousness, shall have their reward with their Lord; on them shall be no fear, nor shall they grieve.' (Surah Al Baqarah, Chapter 2 Verse 62)

God has commanded Muslims in the Qur'an not to insult other faiths. In fact, Christians and Jews are given an honourable title in the Qur'an, 'the people of the Book'.

The Prophet of Allah (pbuh*) said: 'One who kills a non-Muslim person (under the guardianship of an Islamic state) will not even smell the fragrance of Paradise.'

He also said, 'Whoever hurts a non-Muslim person (under the guardianship of an Islamic state), I am his adversary, and I shall be an adversary to him on the Day of Resurrection.'

* Peace be upon him.

⇨ The above information is reprinted with kind permission from Islam is Peace. Visit www.islamispeace.org.uk for more information.

© Islam is Peace

ISLAM IS PEACE

Guantánamo Bay: now's the time for Barack Obama to close it down

The US President promised to shut the prison when he came to office. With bin Laden dead, he should follow through.

By Clare Algar

Barack Obama's first executive order when he was made president called for the closure of Guantánamo Bay as quickly as possible. He didn't follow through immediately when he had the chance – when he was still riding high on his election victory and the world was in love with him. Instead, he tried to work with the Republicans to create a bipartisan solution, an effort which failed dismally.

Now, with the killing of Osama bin Laden, President Obama again has a window in which to close this prison. Indeed, it could even be a shrewd political move, a demonstration to a world which is questioning the legality of bin Laden's killing that the President has a handle on what is right.

Discussion of the legitimacy of bin Laden's killing is somewhat fruitless; we do not have and probably never will have the details. It can be argued that entering into an allied nation's sovereign territory without permission and shooting an unarmed person, even if he is an enemy leader, is both questionable under international law and a disappointing missed opportunity to put one of the most noted terrorists in history in the dock.

But it is at least arguable that it was a legitimate action. Congress's authorisation of use of military force legislation – passed in relation to those responsible for 9/11 – definitely allowed for the use of military force: 'The President is authorised to use all necessary and appropriate force against those nations, organisations or persons he determines planned, authorised, committed, or aided the terrorist attacks that occurred on 11 September 2001, or harboured such organisations or persons, in order to prevent any future acts of international terrorism against the United States by such nations, organisations or persons.'

Maybe President Obama could grasp this opportunity to say: 'We did the right thing here. And also, we have an unlawful prison which contains a bunch of prisoners who have been cleared for release for many years and who are on any view harmless. We are going to do the right thing about that too. I said that we would close it several years ago – now we are actually going to do it. And while I'm at it, I will reaffirm that torture is not the way that civilised nations get their intelligence.'

It would not be easy. Some Republicans are taking this opportunity to tout torture wherever they can. Fox News seems to consider its corporate mission to be the promotion of torture as an intelligence policy. This, despite convincing arguments that the information which led to the capture of bin Laden did not come from torture. Even Donald Rumsfeld said: 'It is true that some information that came from normal interrogation approaches at Guantánamo did lead to information that was beneficial in this instance. But it was not harsh treatment and it was not waterboarding.'

Then there is what to do with the people in Guantánamo. Because Obama did not seize the moment to resettle the Uighers – whose innocence of terrorism is now unchallenged by anyone – in the US, he has now lost any momentum to resettle anyone from Guantánamo in the US. Thus, he has to find allied nations to take the men in order to close the prison.

In addition, there is the money – Congress's National Defense Authorization Act for 2011 contained restrictions on public money being used to bring Guantánamo detainees to the US or transfer them to foreign countries. When he signed this act, Obama said he would 'seek repeal of these restrictions'. This has not happened. Now it is time to do it.

Even without repealing the act, there are some things the Obama administration could do to get the zero threat people out of Guantánamo: when they win their *habeas* litigation, the hearing in which the case against a detainee is brought before a court, the administration could choose not to appeal. They could stop litigating the *habeas* litigation in a mindlessly aggressive way which perpetuates the image of these men as being dangerous. They could negotiate consent orders which would agree to their release.

As I say, it would not be easy, but Barack Obama applied for the job. Everyone has tricky things on their 'to do' list, but this is not you or me. The President is in a pretty good bargaining position – not only is he is the most powerful man in the world, he has incredible popular support now and for the next few weeks. If he were to put sufficient political welly into this, he could close Guantánamo Bay.

This article first appeared in the *Observer*, 8 May 2011.

THE OBSERVER

Guantánamo Bay detainees are not ordinary criminals

Barack Obama's change of mind over the way terror suspects are tried was difficult but right, writes Malcolm Rifkind.

It has turned out to be a case not of 'Yes, we can', but 'No, we can't'. With America's reputation tarnished by images of kneeling, blindfolded prisoners at Guantánamo Bay, and reports of waterboarding, extraordinary rendition and the abuse of detainees in Abu Ghraib, Barack Obama made Guantánamo's closure one of his key campaign pledges.

Upon taking office in January 2009, one of his first executive orders mandated that the jail would be shut within the year. He was also determined to ensure that, wherever possible, detainees would be tried in civilian courts within the United States. Even Khalid Sheikh Mohammed, the mastermind of the 9/11 bombings, was to face a judge and jury, preferably in New York.

> **The fact that there is not sufficient evidence to try them does not mean they are likely to be innocent: the evidence that they are hard, determined terrorists is often overwhelming**

Despite all the President's efforts, however, these pledges have evaporated. Today, Guantánamo remains open. This week it was announced that it will not be civilian courts that will try such detainees, but Bush-era military commissions, which had been suspended for two years. This decision won Mr Obama rare plaudits from his political enemies, but deeply disappointed his own supporters.

How did this happen? The President used every means available to him to get his way, but Congress was unsympathetic from the start; when the mid-term elections delivered the House of Representatives to the Republicans, there was no chance of a change of heart. Nor was public opinion on side: most people were unimpressed with the plan. New Yorkers were so opposed to Khalid Sheikh Mohammed being tried in their city that the idea had been abandoned some time ago.

Does this mean that Obama has lost the moral high ground? Not necessarily. Last week, I discussed these issues with officials in Washington. They are people with high ethical standards, determined that even terrorists will receive proper justice in a civilised manner.

As far back as May 2009, the President had acknowledged that military commissions might still be necessary, but indicated his determination to make the way they operate more consistent with the rule of law. In particular, they would – as with civilian courts – no longer be able to rely on evidence obtained via cruel, inhuman or degrading treatment. Indeed, various sources suggest that a military commission will be able to convict Khalid Sheikh Mohammed without relying on anything he said after being subjected to waterboarding.

Such military commissions should ensure a reasonably fair trial for many of the 172 detainees at Guantánamo. Some of the remainder will be released when they are no longer considered a threat. But the central problem is the hard core – around 48 of the current detainees – who will be neither tried nor released. The fact that there is not sufficient evidence to try them does not mean they are likely to be innocent: the evidence that they are hard, determined terrorists is often overwhelming. But it may have been obtained by covert means, which cannot be revealed without endangering the lives of innocent people, or revealing your surveillance methods, to the benefit of terrorists still at large.

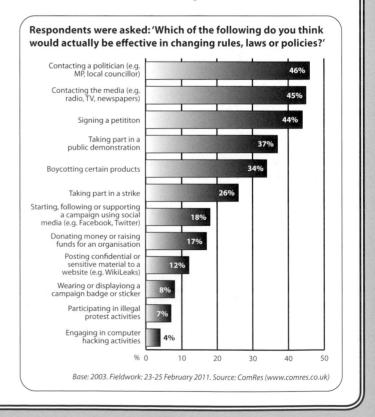

Respondents were asked: 'Which of the following do you think would actually be effective in changing rules, laws or policies?'

Contacting a politician (e.g. MP, local councillor)	46%
Contacting the media (e.g. radio, TV, newspapers)	45%
Signing a petititon	44%
Taking part in a public demonstration	37%
Boycotting certain products	34%
Taking part in a strike	26%
Starting, following or supporting a campaign using social media (e.g. Facebook, Twitter)	18%
Donating money or raising funds for an organisation	17%
Posting confidential or sensitive material to a website (e.g. WikiLeaks)	12%
Wearing or displayiong a campaign badge or sticker	8%
Participating in illegal protest activities	7%
Engaging in computer hacking activities	4%

Base: 2003. Fieldwork: 23-25 February 2011. Source: ComRes (www.comres.co.uk)

The dilemma of how you deal with such people is not just an American problem: European countries face similar issues. To put this in perspective, it is worth remembering that we have in our prisons many murderers who have served very long sentences, but who may never be released, because they are deemed still to represent a threat to the public.

> **We may have to steel ourselves to the need to incarcerate these few individuals in our midst who are, or would be, mass murderers, in order to prevent them from carrying out their evil purpose**

Of course, these are prisoners who have been tried and convicted, not detained without trial – but the majority will have murdered at most a handful of people. Yet some of those in Guantánamo, or elsewhere, have murdered – or been trained to murder – hundreds or even thousands of innocent people. If it is thought certain that they would try to commit such atrocities if released, should the acceptability of their incarceration be judged by the same criteria as we apply to 'ordinary' crime?

This is a far more serious issue than the question of whether suspects should be detained for 14 or 28 days. We are talking here about terrorists who have been trained to kill hundreds, where the evidence against them may be very strong. And we may have to steel ourselves to the need to incarcerate these few individuals in our midst who are, or would be, mass murderers, in order to prevent them from carrying out their evil purpose.

To that end, President Obama's proposals are sensible. He argues that such persons must be detained in civilised and acceptable conditions. Their cases must be reviewed regularly to ensure that the threat that they represent is still present. These reviews should be carried out by judges, with full access to all the information, and entirely independent of the Government.

For the President's original supporters, it may never be 'glad confident morning again', to quote Robert Browning's attack on Wordsworth for deserting the liberal cause. Yet we should still have some sympathy for the President, for taking a difficult but necessary decision – and remember that his dilemma is one faced by all civilised nations.

Sir Malcolm Rifkind MP is chairman of the Parliamentary Intelligence and Security Committee and a former Foreign Secretary.
8 March 2011

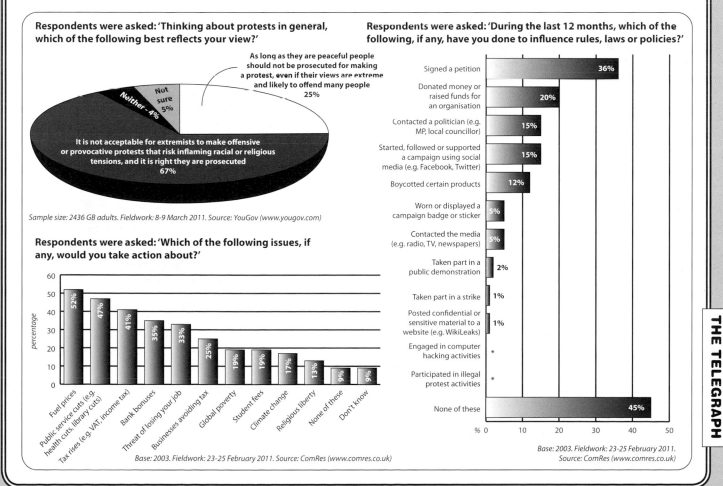

Respondents were asked: 'Thinking about protests in general, which of the following best reflects your view?'

As long as they are peaceful people should not be prosecuted for making a protest, even if their views are extreme and likely to offend many people
25%

Not sure 5%

Neither - 4%

It is not acceptable for extremists to make offensive or provocative protests that risk inflaming racial or religious tensions, and it is right they are prosecuted
67%

Sample size: 2436 GB adults. Fieldwork: 8-9 March 2011. Source: YouGov (www.yougov.com)

Respondents were asked: 'Which of the following issues, if any, would you take action about?'

- Fuel prices — 52%
- Public service cuts (e.g. health cuts, library cuts) — 47%
- Tax rises (e.g. VAT, income tax) — 41%
- Bank bonuses — 35%
- Threat of losing your job — 33%
- Businesses avoiding tax — 25%
- Global poverty — 19%
- Student fees — 19%
- Climate change — 17%
- Religious liberty — 13%
- None of these — 9%
- Don't know — 9%

Base: 2003. Fieldwork: 23-25 February 2011. Source: ComRes (www.comres.co.uk)

Respondents were asked: 'During the last 12 months, which of the following, if any, have you done to influence rules, laws or policies?'

- Signed a petition — 36%
- Donated money or raised funds for an organisation — 20%
- Contacted a politician (e.g. MP, local councillor) — 15%
- Started, followed or supported a campaign using social media (e.g. Facebook, Twitter) — 15%
- Boycotted certain products — 12%
- Worn or displayed a campaign badge or sticker — 5%
- Contacted the media (e.g. radio, TV, newspapers) — 5%
- Taken part in a public demonstration — 2%
- Taken part in a strike — 1%
- Posted confidential or sensitive material to a website (e.g. WikiLeaks) — 1%
- Engaged in computer hacking activities — *
- Participated in illegal protest activities — *
- None of these — 45%

Base: 2003. Fieldwork: 23-25 February 2011. Source: ComRes (www.comres.co.uk)

Testimonies from detainees

Information from Amnesty International.

'They put me in a kneeling position like this. They told me not to sit back on my heels. They said: "look straight ahead, don't look to the sides". There were four or five guys surrounding me and insulting me and beating me. For three days, I was not allowed to sleep. Then, on the fourth, they made me kneel all night. They punched me, they kicked me, once to my chin.

'Another time I was told to lie down and they picked me up by my neck so I was half-strangled and they said: "we are going to kill you unless you confess what you did".'

Detainee, Afghanistan

'The Americans interrogated us on our first night which we coined as "the black night". They cut our clothes with scissors, left us naked and took photos of us before they gave us Afghan clothes to wear. They then handcuffed our hands behind our backs, blindfolded us and started interrogating us. The interrogator was an Egyptian. He asked me about the names of all members of my family, relatives and friends. They threatened me with death, accusing me of belonging to al-Qaeda.

'They put us in an underground cell measuring approximately two metres by three metres. There were ten of us in the cell. We spent three months in the cell. There was no room for us to sleep so we had to alternate. The window of the cell was very small. It was too hot in the cell, despite the fact that outside the temperature was freezing (there was snow), because the cell was overcrowded. They used to open the cell from time to time to allow air in.

'During the three-month period in the cell we were not allowed outside into the open air. We were allowed access to toilets twice a day; the toilets were located by the cell.' Walid al-Qadasi said that the prisoners were only fed once a day and that loud music was used as torture. He said that one of his fellow detainees went insane. Walid al-Qadasi was eventually transferred to Bagram, where he faced a month of interrogation.

Testimony of former detainee given to Amnesty April 2004, Yemen. Detention in Kabul

He stated that he was blindfolded, kicked and beaten, and had his clothes removed. 'Then they asked me which animals I had had sexual activities with – they made the noise of goats, sheep, dogs, cows. They laughed at me. I said that such actions were against our Afghan and Islamic tradition, but they again asked me which kind of animals do you want to have sex with? Then they beat me with a stick from the back and kicked me. I still have pains in my back as a result.'

Former detainee, Afghanistan, July 2003

'I was hooded while being taken to interrogation and some of the time during interrogation. I was interrogated at least three or four times a week for up to seven or eight hours a day. Sometimes I was just left sitting in the interrogation tent with nothing, no food or toilet facilities.

'The guards in Kandahar regularly tore up the Qur'an and threw it around. My body hair was shaved, including my pubic hair. After three months in Kandahar I was flown to Guantánamo Bay, Cuba, on 1 May 2002. I was stripped naked, given a full body search and pictures were taken of me naked.'

Statement of former detainee given during legal proceedings in Kandahar

Mr Al Dossari was arrested in Pakistan and held by Pakistani authorities for several weeks. Mr Al Dossari was transferred from Pakistan to Kandahar, Afghanistan, via airplane by the US authorities. On the plane, he was shackled by chains on his thighs, waist and shoulders, with his hands tied behind him.

The chains were so tight around his shoulders that he was forced to lean forward at an extreme angle during the entire flight. This caused great pain to Mr Al Dossari's stomach, where he had had an operation some years before. When Mr Al Dossari complained about the pain, he was hit and kicked in the stomach, causing him to vomit blood.

Upon arriving in Kandahar, Mr Al Dossari and other detainees were put in a row on the ground in a tent. US Marines urinated on the detainees and put cigarettes out on them (Mr Al Dossari has scars that are consistent with those that would be caused by cigarette burns). A US soldier pushed Mr Al Dossari's head into the ground violently and other soldiers walked on him.

Mohammad Al Dossari has alleged, among other things, that he was forced to walk barefoot over barbed wire and that his head was pushed to the ground on broken glass. He has alleged that US soldiers subjected him to electric shocks, death threats, assault and humiliation.

Guantánamo detainee. Unclassified details of the alleged treatment of Bahraini detainee Jumâah Mohammad Abdul Latif Al Dossari, as provided to Amnesty by the US lawyers for the detainees

All indicated that they had been horribly treated, particularly in Afghanistan and Pakistan where they were first held for many months after being taken into custody (in Kandahar, Kohat, Bagram). Although the words they used were different, the stories they told were remarkably similar – terrible beatings, hung from wrists and beaten, removal of clothes, hooding, naked exposure to extreme cold, paraded naked in front of female guards, sexual taunting by both male and female guards/interrogators,

AMNESTY INTERNATIONAL

some sexual abuse (rectal intrusion), being kept in uncomfortable positions for hours.

All confirmed that this treatment was by Americans. Several said pictures were taken of some of this abuse. Some of the pictures still exist and are being used by the interrogators. Many knew that the Americans had killed several people during the interrogations at these places. Several also mentioned the use of electric shocks – like ping pong paddles put under arms – some had this done; many saw it done. Several said they just could not believe Americans could act this way.

The handwritten notes of a US lawyer who met with Kuwaiti detainees in Guantánamo in January 2005

According to his account, recorded by a lawyer who visited him in Guantánamo in early 2005, Omar went for seven to eight days without food in Bagram. He was held in a dark room for days on end, without any access to light. Omar and others were locked in boxes with no air and effectively suffocated for long periods.

He was chained to the wall, with his hands high up in the Strappado position. This caused extreme pain. While he was in Bagram, as part of the humiliation process, Omar was forced to live naked for long periods. His hands and feet were tied so tightly, they swelled to much above normal size. He was forced to move and assume uncomfortable positions while tied this way. He was often beaten with chains. He was also forced to stay in positions and to urinate and defecate on himself.

Libyan national and UK resident Omar Deghayes

'I reached Bangkok International Airport on 6 July 2003 and at the airport I was illegally and immorally arrested – back hand/leg cuffed, a black big mask on my head up to neck, was thrown on floor of station wagon facing down. I am heart patient/diabetic/high blood pressure/skin disorder/gout; it could have been fatal, there was no human consideration at all.

'From the airport I was taken to unknown place for few days and kept eyes covered, ears cover, handcuffed, leg cuffed. After a few days I was transported by plane to Afghanistan, under extremely severe, bad conditions. I was kept in isolation from July 2003 to 20 September 2004 and since then I am in isolation cell in Guantánamo Bay Island. Am I being considered human being or animal, or is USA my God?'

In a handwritten letter to the Combatant Status Review Tribunal (CSRT), dated 8 December 2004, Pakistan national Saifullah Paracha wrote of his abduction by US agents in Thailand and his transportation to Afghanistan, where he was held for more than a year before being transferred to Guantánamo, where he remains

'When they came and arrested and handcuffed me, they were wearing all black. They even covered their heads black. They took me, covered me, put me in a vehicle and sent me somewhere. I don't know where. It was at night. Then from there to the airport right away. We were in a room like this with about eight men. All with covered up faces. They cut off my clothes. They were pulling on my hands and my legs.

'They put me in an airplane and they made me wear the handcuffs that go around your body so I would not do anything on the airplane. This is all kidnapping. Yes. They took me underground in the dark. I did not see light for two weeks, Bagram, Afghanistan. Right there in the dark. They put me in the dark. I was surprised.

'I did not know what I did wrong or what I did. They starved me; they handcuffed me, there was no food, I was under their control. They are the ones who took me and put me there. They know what they have done. I was surprised that the Americans would do such a thing. It shocked me.'

At his hearing in front of the CSRT in Guantánamo on 9 October 2004, Jordanian national and UK resident Jamil El Banna recalled his transfer from Gambia to Afghanistan in what he described as a 'kidnapping' by US agents

⇨ The above information is reprinted with kind permission from Amnesty International. Visit www.amnesty.org.uk for more information.

AMNESTY INTERNATIONAL

The United Kingdom fails on diplomatic assurances

Amnesty International's preliminary response to the UK counter-terrorism review.

Amnesty International has condemned the recommendation of yesterday's UK Home Office review of counter-terrorism and security powers that supports and seeks to extend the use of diplomatic assurances in order to return individuals to countries where they risk being tortured. The findings and recommendations of the UK Home Office counter-terrorism review were announced before Parliament by Theresa May, the Home Secretary, on 26 January.

Amnesty International deplores the UK's continued reliance on diplomatic assurances to deport people to countries where they are at real risk of torture

The UK Home Office review of six key counter-terrorism and security powers, including the use of diplomatic assurances to deport people accused of terrorism-related activity, rejected submissions from human rights organisations, including Amnesty International, that such 'no torture' promises from governments of countries where torture and ill-treatment are systematic or widespread are inherently unreliable and do not sufficiently protect against torture and other ill-treatment.

Amnesty International deplores the UK's continued reliance on diplomatic assurances to deport people to countries where they are at real risk of torture.

The UK has been Europe's most aggressive and influential proponent of these dangerous deals, which are unreliable and unenforceable.

The UK Government has sought to deport foreign nationals accused of terrorism-related activity by a variety of means, to a number of states with poor human rights records. To date, the UK has formal 'memoranda of understanding' (MoUs) with Lebanon, Jordan, Libya and Ethiopia which contain assurances regarding the treatment of such deportees.

The UK has also negotiated bilateral assurances with the Algerian Government on a case-by-case basis to cover individual deportations. In recent months, the UK Government has additionally sought to deport individuals suspected of terrorism-related activity to Pakistan.

The UK Home Office review asserted that monitoring arrangements with local human rights organisations in countries such as Ethiopia would ensure that any mistreatment would be quickly identified and would enable the UK to raise its concerns about mistreatment with the country in question.

Amnesty International considers that no system of post-return monitoring of individuals will render assurances an acceptable alternative to rigorous respect for the absolute prohibition of deportations to risk of torture or other ill-treatment. The organisation stated that the UK Government's position ignores the experience and concerns of international human rights organisations.

The Home Office review fundamentally fails to appreciate the context in which torture and other ill-treatment occurs in states where such practices are systematic or widespread. The climate of secrecy, impunity and deniability in such situations leads to inherent deficiencies in assurances that prevent them from effectively and reliably mitigating against the risk of torture and ill-treatment.

Further, as even the review conceded, where an assurance is breached it is simply left to the governments involved to voluntarily assume responsibility for investigating the breach and hold perpetrators to account. Neither government is likely to wish to acknowledge, especially in any formal or public way, that their actions have led to the torture or other abuse of a prisoner. Relying only on the good faith of the states implicated also compromises the ability of any such torture victim to secure his or her right to reparation and redress, and ignores the fact that, even leaving aside physical consequences, the psychological harm to a person who has been subjected to torture can never fully be repaired.

The use of 'diplomatic assurances' by European countries has been criticised by a number of intergovernmental bodies, including a number of United Nations special procedures, and committees of the Parliamentary Assembly of the Council of Europe and the European Parliament, who have expressly called on member states to refrain from using diplomatic assurances against torture and other ill-treatment.

The UK counter-terrorism review further proposed the eventual repeal of the current 'control orders' regime as specified in the Prevention of Terrorism Act 2005 (PTA), which has been controversially used as an alternative to prosecution or deportation of UK terror suspects who have not been charged with any criminal offence. The Home Secretary outlined proposals for a new regime of administrative measures similar to control orders, though promising that the possible length of curfew periods would be reduced and that certain other restrictions would no longer be used. The renewed scheme the UK Government is proposing retains, however, a variety of measures that will significantly restrict the individuals' rights to liberty, privacy, association, expression and movement. Examples of the measures that are proposed to be available without criminal trial include: the power to order people to spend eight to ten hours every night without leaving their residence (unless they obtain prior permission from the Government to spend particular nights away); forcing people to wear an electronic tag that allows the Government to monitor their movements; forcing disclosure of Internet passwords; prohibiting contact with other named individuals; and regularly reporting to police. According to the proposals, a breach of these restrictions could itself, however, lead to a criminal conviction and sentence of up to five years in prison.

The Home Office review fundamentally fails to appreciate the context in which torture and other ill-treatment occurs in states where such practices are systematic or widespread

The proposals do not provide any detail about the Government's intentions with respect to one of the most controversial aspects of the existing control order regime: the consequences of allowing the use of secret evidence that neither the person subject to the proceeding or his or her lawyer is ever shown, for the right to fair trial. The review implies such controversial procedures will be retained, with some changes, but defers any discussion of specific changes to a later Green Paper on the use of sensitive material in judicial proceedings.

Amnesty International believes that if people will still face the consequences of being labelled 'suspected terrorists' and subjected to special restrictions on their lives, without a fair trial that includes a chance to know the allegations against them in enough detail to have a real chance of challenging the Government's case, this would not be consistent with respect for human rights.

In making the announcement, the Home Secretary announced that the current control orders regimes under the PTA would be renewed until the end of 2011. Amnesty International has called for the immediate repeal of the PTA since its inception, and is disappointed that almost six years later, the so-called temporary legislation remains in place.

The Home Office review also examined stop and search powers under Section 44 of the Terrorism Act 2000, the length of pre-charge detention, the use of communications data including under the Regulation of Investigatory Powers Act 2000 and measures to deal with organisations that promote hatred or violence. Amnesty International is currently assessing the full recommendations of the review in detail.

27 January 2011

⇨ The above information is reprinted with kind permission from Amnesty International UK. Visit www.amnesty.org for more information.

© Amnesty International UK

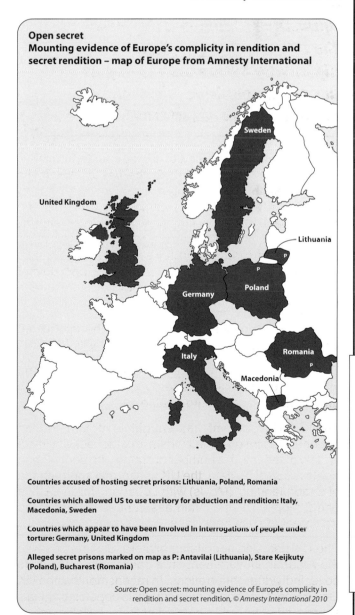

Open secret
Mounting evidence of Europe's complicity in rendition and secret rendition – map of Europe from Amnesty International

Countries accused of hosting secret prisons: Lithuania, Poland, Romania

Countries which allowed US to use territory for abduction and rendition: Italy, Macedonia, Sweden

Countries which appear to have been involved in interrogations of people under torture: Germany, United Kingdom

Alleged secret prisons marked on map as P: Antavilai (Lithuania), Stare Keijkuty (Poland), Bucharest (Romania)

Source: Open secret: mounting evidence of Europe's complicity in rendition and secret rendition, © Amnesty International 2010

⇨ Having extreme thoughts or beliefs is not a crime. Using unlawful force or threats to support a belief or ideology is. (page 1)

⇨ Riots and malicious damage, sabotage and disruption, revolutions and assassinations: political violence in one shape or another has been with us since the earliest days of civilisation. (page 2)

⇨ Five years on from the 7 July 2005 terrorist attack on the London Underground, known as '7/7', more than half (53%) of the UK's population think that the threat of terrorism has stayed at the same level, with older people feeling slightly more worried than their younger counterparts. (page 4)

⇨ According to START's Global Terrorism Database (GTD), Great Britain (England, Wales and Scotland) has been the target of 604 terrorist attacks since 1970. (page 5)

⇨ Between 1970 and 1999, almost two-thirds of all terrorist attacks in Great Britain with a known perpetrator were the responsibility of the Irish Republican Army or a related Irish nationalist splinter group, responsible for 293 attacks or 64% of terrorist activity in Great Britain during this period. (page 6)

⇨ In Great Britain, businesses – not transportation infrastructure – have traditionally been the favoured targets of terrorists, with 38% of British attacks from 1970 through to 2008 directed against private businesses. In contrast, only 7% of terrorist incidents have attacked British transportation targets during this period – a total of 44 such attacks. (page 7)

⇨ The Security Service estimates that over 2,000 people in the UK pose a terrorist threat and in March 2005 it was estimated that there were up to 200 al-Qaeda-trained operatives in the UK. (page 8)

⇨ Almost half of all secondary school headteachers have contacted the police for advice on combating violent extremism, according to new Government-commissioned research. (page 12)

⇨ Universities have more of a problem with animal rights extremists than Islamist radicals, according to an official report that has been criticised for failing to recognise the depth of the problem. (page 13)

⇨ The Independent Monitoring Commission reported in November 2010 that Republican terrorist groups continued to pose a substantial and potentially lethal threat. The groups continue to carry out attacks on the security forces in Northern Ireland. (page 14)

⇨ Only one in four terror suspects were charged with a terrorism-related offence in 2010, figures showed. A total of 130 people were arrested on suspicion of being involved in terrorism in the 12 months to September 2010, but only 36 were charged with a terror-related offence. (page 27)

⇨ Over 101,000 people were stopped under Section 44 of the Terrorism Act in the year ending May 2010, without a single arrest for anything terrorism-related, and over 85,000 people were stopped under Schedule 7, which governs ports and airports. (page 28)

⇨ 25% of people surveyed viewed Islam as a dangerous religion which incites violence. 21% considered that violence or terrorism on the part of some Muslims is unsurprising given the actions of the West in the Muslim world and the hostility towards Muslims in Britain. (page 31)

⇨ In Arabic, the word 'jihad' means to strive, struggle and exert effort. It is a central and broad Islamic concept that primarily means to struggle against evil inclinations within oneself. (page 32)

⇨ There are 172 detainees being held at the Guantánamo Bay facility. (page 34)

⇨ The UK Government has sought to deport foreign nationals accused of terrorism-related activity by a variety of means, to a number of states with poor human rights records. To date, the UK has formal 'memoranda of understanding' (MoUs) with Lebanon, Jordan, Libya and Ethiopia which contain assurances regarding the treatment of such deportees. (page 38)

The 7/7 bombings

Also know as the London bombings, this refers to the events of 7 July 2005, when four suicide bombers took the lives of 56 people on the London transport system. The incident was the deadliest single act of terrorism in the UK since Lockerbie (the 1988 bombing of Pan Am Flight 103 which killed 270), and the deadliest bombing in London since the Second World War. The attacks were significant in drawing UK attention to the terrorism problem – they demonstrated that terrorism could occur at home as well as abroad, and could even be perpetrated by British citizens (three of the four bombers were British).

9/11

9/11 is a common way of referring to the events of 11 September 2001, the date on which four passenger planes were hijacked by Al-Qaeda militants and flown into US targets – notably the twin towers of the World Trade Center in New York – causing thousands of lives to be lost. These attacks were significant in bringing terrorism into the international spotlight, changing the world's political climate and launching the 'War on Terror'.

Al-Qaeda

Al-Qaeda is a global network of Sunni Islamist terrorist cells, founded by Osama bin Laden in the late 1980s. The group has been responsible for attacks on numerous civilian and military targets, taking responsibility for, among others, 9/11 and the 2002 Bali bombings.

Animal rights extremists

Animal rights extremists object to the exploitation of animals by human beings, and in recent years their particular focus has been the use of animals in medical tests by pharmaceutical companies. Extremists have been known to use tactics including death threats, planting bombs and destroying property against pharmaceutical workers and their families.

Counter-terrorism

Counter-terrorism refers to the tactics and techniques used by governments and other groups to prevent or minimise a terrorist threat.

Extraordinary rendition

Rendition is the arrest and transference of a fugitive from one country or state to another and is an acceptable legal practice. When it takes place without the approval of a judicial authority, however, or where the suspect is afterwards tortured in breach of their human rights, it is known as 'extraordinary rendition'. The USA has been accused of this practice with the alleged complicity of other Western nations, including the UK.

Extremism

Extremism refers to beliefs or practices that are seen as radical, and can give rise to militance. Groups justifying their violence on Islamic grounds, such as Al-Qaeda or Hamas, often come to mind first, but Christianity, Judaism and Hinduism have all given rise to their own forms of militant extremism.

The Good Friday Agreement

Also called the Belfast or Stormont Agreement, this was a major breakthrough in the Northern Ireland peace process. On 10 April 1998, documents were signed which set out to change the relationships between political parties in Northern Ireland, and between Northern Ireland, the Republic of Ireland and the United Kingdom.

Guantánamo Bay detention camp

A detainment facility in Cuba established by the George Bush-led US Government in 2002 to hold prisoners from the wars in Iraq and Afghanistan. The existence of the facility is controversial due to its secretive nature, allegations of mistreatment of prisoners and human rights abuses, and the fact that detainees are denied a fair trial. Although the current US President, Barack Obama, has previously pledged to close the facility, steps in this direction have yet to be taken.

The Taliban

A militant Islamist group which ruled large parts of Afghanistan between 1996 and 2001.

Terrorism

The word 'terrorism' dates back to the 18th century, but there is no globally accepted definition of the term. The most widely accepted is probably that put forward by the US State Department, which states that terrorism is 'premeditated, politically motivated violence perpetrated against non-combatant targets by subnational groups or clandestine agents, usually intended to influence an audience.' Types include Nationalist-Separatist, Religious, Right-Wing and Left-Wing Terrorism.

Afghanistan conflict after death of bin Laden 24–5
age of terrorists 9
al-Qaeda
  and Afghanistan conflict 24–5
  after death of Osama bin Laden 23
  terrorist attacks in Great Britain 6
Amnesty International response to UK counter-terrorism
  review 38–9
anti-terrorism *see* counter-terrorism
Anti-terrorism Crime and Security Act 2001 19
arrest powers, Terrorism Act 16

bin Laden, Osama, effect of death on al-Qaeda 23

children as suicide bombers 11–12
Continuity IRA (CIRA) 14
convictions for terrorism 9–10
coordinated terrorist attacks 6
counter-terrorism 15–25
  legislation 15–16, 19, 20
    and liberty 26–7
  police powers 15–16
  Prevent strategy 17–18
  review 21–2, 26, 38–9
Counter Terrorism Act 2008 19

detention of suspects, Terrorism Act 16

education and employment status of terrorists 9
extremism
  in schools 12
  in universities 13–14

Great Britain *see* United Kingdom
Guantánamo Bay 33–5
  torture of detainees 36–7

headteachers, concern about extremism 12

inter-faith relations, public attitudes to 30–31
Irish Republican terrorist groups 14
Islam 32
  public attitudes to 4, 30–31
  see also Muslims
Islamist terrorism 8–10

jihad 32
July 7 terrorist attacks 4, 5

legislation, anti-terrorism 19, 20
liberty versus security 26–7
London bombings 4, 5

Muslims
  public attitudes to 4, 30–31
  as stop and search targets 28–9
  see also Islam

nationality of UK terrorists 9

Obama, Barack, and closure of Guantánamo Bay 33,
  34–5

police powers, Terrorism Act 16
Prevent strategy 17–18
Prevention of Terrorism Act 2005 19
proscribed organisations 15–16, 19
  Islamic 10
public attitudes
  following London bombings 4
  to inter-faith relations 30–31
public transport
  effects of London bombings 4
  as terrorism targets 7

radicalism at universities 13–14
Real IRA (RIRA) 14
reasons for terrorism 1
religions, public attitudes to 30–31
religious tolerance and Islam 32
RIRA (Real IRA) 14

schools, concerns about extremism 12
search of premises, police powers 16
Secret Organisation of al-Qaeda , London bombings 6
sentences for terrorist offences 9–10, 19
stop and search
  anti-Muslim discrimination 28–9
  Terrorism Act 16
suicide terrorism
  Great Britain 5–6
  use of children 11–12

tackling terrorism 15–25
Taliban, using children as suicide bombers 11–12
terror-related arrests 27
terrorism
  changes 2–3
  definition 1, 15
  effects 2–3
  reasons for 1
Terrorism Act 2000 15–16, 19
Terrorism Act 2006 19
terrorism offences 16
Terrorism Prevention and Investigation Measures Bill 20
terrorist attacks in UK 5–7
  effect on the public 4
  Irish Republican groups 14
  Islamist 8–10
terrorist training camps and Islamic terrorism 10
terrorists, profiles 9
torture by US soldiers 36–7
transport systems *see* public transport

United Kingdom

counter-terrorism review 21–2, 38–9
counter-terrorism strategy 17–18
Islamist terrorism 8–10
terrorist attacks 5–7
universities and extremism 13–14

US soldiers, torture of prisoners 36–7

violent extremism
  in schools 12
  in universities 13–14

ACKNOWLEDGEMENTS

The publisher is grateful for permission to reproduce the following material.

While every care has been taken to trace and acknowledge copyright, the publisher tenders its apology for any accidental infringement or where copyright has proved untraceable. The publisher would be pleased to come to a suitable arrangement in any such case with the rightful owner.

Chapter One: Terror and Violent Extremism

Terrorist or extremist activity, © Metropolitan Police Authority 2011, *The changing face of terrorism,* © Lloyd's, *7/7: five years on,* © YouGov, *On the fifth anniversary of the 7/7 London transit attack,* © National Consortium for the Study of Terrorism and Responses to Terrorism (START), College Park MD, 2010, *Islamist terrorism,* © Robin Simcox, Hannah Stuart and Houriya Ahmed, Islamist Terrorism: The British Connections (Centre for Social Cohesion, 2010), *Groomed for suicide: how Taliban recruits children for mass murder,* © Guardian News and Media Limited 2011, *Half of secondary heads seek police help on violent extremism,* © TES Connect, *Animal rights extremists 'more of a problem than Islamists',* © Telegraph Media Group Limited 2011, *Irish Republican terrorist groups,* © Crown copyright is reproduced with the permission of Her Majesty's Stationery Office.

Chapter Two: Tackling Terrorism

Anti-terrorism powers, © Liberty, *Should Britain work with 'extremists' to prevent terrorism?,* © openDemocracy, *The Terrorism Acts – the facts,* © SACC, *Terrorism Prevention and Investigation Measures Bill,* © Crown copyright is reproduced with the permission of Her Majesty's Stationery Office, *The counter-terrorism review,* © openDemocracy, *Al-Qaeda will seek revenge,* © Guardian News and Media Limited 2011, *Victory in the war on terror is now within the West's reach,* © Telegraph Media Group Limited 2011.

Chapter Three: Liberty vs Security

Stop trying to balance liberty with security, © spiked, *Only one in four terror suspects charged,* © Press Association, *Stop and search figures 'hide evidence of systematic anti-Muslim discrimination',* © Islamic Human Rights Commission (IHRC), *Searchlight on religion,* © University of Manchester, *Misconceptions about Islam and terrorism,* © Islam is Peace, *Guantánamo Bay: now's the time for Barack Obama to close it down,* © Guardian News and Media Limited 2011, *Guantánamo Bay detainees are not ordinary criminals,* © Telegraph Media Group Limited 2011, *Testimonies from detainees,* © Amnesty International, *The United Kingdom fails on diplomatic assurances,* © Amnesty International UK.

Illustrations

Pages 2, 15, 29, 37: Don Hatcher; pages 4, 21, 26, 32: Simon Kneebone; pages 8, 17, 25, 31: Angelo Madrid; pages 10, 23: Bev Aisbett.

Cover photography

Left: © Thomas Gray. Centre: © Michael Foran. Right: © Elly Waterman.

Additional acknowledgements

With thanks to the Independence team: Mary Chapman, Sandra Dennis and Jan Sunderland.

Lisa Firth
Cambridge
September, 2011

ASSIGNMENTS

The following tasks aim to help you think through the issues surrounding terrorism and provide a better understanding of the topic.

1 'One man's terrorist is another man's freedom fighter.' Discuss your views on the meaning behind this phrase and summarise your thoughts in the form of an essay, referring to at least two historical or current figures in your answer: for example, Malcolm X, Nelson Mandela, Martin McGuinness.

2 Find out about the WikiLeaks website and the information it has previously released about extraordinary rendition Do you think it was right to release this information? Do the public have a right to know about suspected human rights abuses, or is there a danger such leaks could compromise national security? Discuss your views with a partner.

3 Find out more about the case of the Birmingham Six, six men imprisoned for life in 1975 for the Birmingham pub bombings carried out by the Provisional IRA. Write a summary of their case. In what way can it inform our treatment of terrorist suspects today?

4 Look at a satirical news website such as The Daily Mash (www.thedailymash.co.uk), or use a site such as YouTube to watch clips from satirical programmes like Have I Got News For You. How do programmes and websites like these, whose primary purpose is to entertain, cover traumatic topics from the news such as terrorist attacks without seeming callous? Find and compare some examples and write a review.

5 Read 'The Islamist' by Ed Husain, covering the five years the author spent as an Islamic fundamentalist. Why is Husain drawn to fundamentalism initially, and why does he later become disillusioned? Write a review of the book.

6 'One who would trade liberty for security deserves neither.' Use this quote, often attributed to Benjamin Franklin, as the starting point for an essay discussing the conflict between counter-terrorism and civil liberties.

7 Do you think it is right that Emdadur Choudhury, a Muslim extremist who burned poppies during a protest on Armistice Day, was prosecuted? What about Terry Jones, the US pastor who was prevented from burning copies of the Qur'an? Should peaceful protests be allowed regardless of how offensive they might be deemed, or should those which could inflame racial or religious tensions be banned?

8 Watch the comedy film 'Four Lions'. Do you think it is right to use the actions of suicide bombers as the basis for a comedy? Do you feel the film handled its subject matter in a sensitive way? How did you feel towards the four main characters by the end of the film? Discuss your feelings about the film in small groups.

9 Find out about the history of the conflict in Northern Ireland commonly referred to as 'the Troubles', and how it has impacted on the UK as a whole in the 20th century particularly. How did the Good Friday Agreement to some extent resolve the conflict? Was it right for the British Government to deal with extremists in this situation, if the result was an end to conflict? Write a summary of your research and conclusions.

10 'This house believes it is never acceptable to use torture to gain evidence of terrorism, no matter what the circumstances.' Debate this motion in two groups, with one group arguing in favour and the other against.

11 Do you think it is ever right for governments to use extraordinary rendition? Discuss your views in groups of three, playing 'devil's advocate' where necessary in order to develop your debate.

12 Find out about the Human Rights Act 1998, which introduced some of the rights enshrined in the Universal Declaration of Human Rights into British domestic law. Some people feel that this act should be repealed. Why do you think they might feel that way? What are your views?

13 'If civil liberties have to be sacrificed to keep us safe then that is just a price we will have to pay. Those who have nothing to fear have nothing to hide.' Do you agree with this view? Write an essay presenting the case for and against this viewpoint and giving your own conclusions. Use articles from Chapter Three to help you.

14 A right-wing extremist who planted bombs near Government buildings in Oslo in July 2011 before massacring 69 young people on a summer camp has received a lot of media attention for his views and motives. Do you think it is important for terrorists and their actions to be analysed if we are to prevent future attacks, or is this merely giving them what they want?